TRANSITIONING
TO A VEGAN DIET

(WITHOUT GIVING UP YOUR FAVORITE FOODS)

B.W. LEETE

ISBN - 9781701382022

DISCLAIMER

This book is for educational and entertainment purposes only. The author is not a nutritionist, fitness professional or medical professional. The views expressed in this book are those of the author alone and should not be taken as expert instruction. While all attempts have been made to verify the information in this publication, neither the author nor the publisher assumes any responsibility for errors, omissions, or the reader's interpretations of the subject matter.

Any perceived slight of any individual, business, or organization is purely unintentional.

For Candace

CONTENTS

Why Vegan?

Why do you want to go vegan? There are many different reasons people choose to adopt a vegan diet. Many people go vegan because they love animals and wish to live a nonviolent, compassionate lifestyle. Some go vegan for their own health—perhaps they've suffered from a particular ailment and have heard or read that a plant-based diet has helped others facing the same health problems. Some adopt a vegan lifestyle because they disapprove of industrial agriculture and its impact on world hunger, the environment, and climate change. People may switch to veganism because it's affordable and meat is generally considered a luxury food item in many parts of the world. Some people go vegan simply because they don't like the taste of meat and other animal products. Others do it for the animals, or for any combination of these reasons.

A person's reasons for going vegan can change over time, with many who initially made the switch for their own health claiming that they later began caring more about the suffering of animals in the meat production industry. On the other side of the spectrum, some people who adopted a vegan lifestyle solely for the animals have later become more concerned about their own personal health, perhaps even shifting from a junk food vegan diet to a whole foods plant-based approach. The reasons people cite for going vegan can change over time, but the definition of a vegan remains the same: someone who actively abstains from eating or using products derived from animals whenever possible.

Whatever the reason a person may decide to go vegan, the shift presents a drastic change in both how they eat and how they live. In many cases, the ways in which people think, feel, and communicate are also affected. When a newbie vegan uses a phrase such as "more than one way to skin a cat" after going vegan, he or she may be hit with the hard truth that living a vegan lifestyle runs much deeper than merely not eating animals and not wearing their skin or fur. The way humans perceive animals as inferior beings, as objects or property permeates virtually every aspect of our lives. Veganism is about more than changing our diets. It's about changing our lives for the better.

Different, Not Difficult

In The Easy Way to Stop Smoking, author Allen Carr postulates that smoking cessation is only difficult because the prevailing belief is that it's difficult. If a person trying to quit smoking focuses only on how hard it is, on how much they miss their precious cigarettes, on how they'll never be able to enjoy their morning coffee or their commute to work without a cigarette, *of course* it's going to be hard. On the other hand, if that person focuses on how good they're going to feel when their lungs begin to heal, on how much energy they're going to have, on how much money they'll be saving, and on how greatly improved their quality of life will be, they've shifted to a positive mindset. Focusing only on the benefits of smoking cessation, rather than on how difficult it is to part with their dear friend Nicotine, will make the process immeasurably easier.

The lives of non-smokers aren't inherently more stressful or troublesome because they're lacking the wonderful benefit of cigarettes—and for anyone who thinks quitting smoking is hard, think of how hard it was to *start* smoking! The coughing, gagging, and choking that persists until the lungs have reluctantly adapted to the toxic smoke and the addiction begins to take hold. Quitting smoking isn't necessarily any tougher than starting to smoke. They're both new and different, and it takes time for the body and mind to adjust to the changes.

Similarly, going vegan may be tough for anyone who places their focus on what they're "giving up" by holding onto thoughts like: "*How am I going to live without cheese?*" "*I'm giving up all my favorite foods!*" "*I'll never be able to eat a cheeseburger again!*" "*I'd rather die than live without steak!*" Many people refuse to consider going vegan because their prevailing thoughts are focused on all the things they think they'd be sacrificing. In addition to those negative thoughts, many people also hold the belief that vegans are weak, sick, malnourished, and alienated from society. They may also think vegans aren't truly making any sort of impact, that their choices and actions aren't helping animals or the planet. Considering all these common misconceptions, it's no wonder more people don't adopt a vegan lifestyle. Who would want to adopt a difficult lifestyle that that drains all their willpower and offers no perceived benefits?

As quitting smoking is generally regarded as difficult, so is going vegan, but the difficulty lies only in the mindset and the fact that it's different from what most people are used to. The being different part is easy to overcome. Humans are incredibly adaptable creatures and adjusting to changes in diet is generally the easy part. The hard part is shifting perception. A person trying out a vegan diet who focuses only on how much they miss pizza, hamburgers, and ice cream will struggle with the changes in their diet and lifestyle much more than a person who is looking forward to eating a vegan pizza, making black bean burgers at home, and trying out Ben & Jerry's non-dairy flavors.

A newbie vegan who is *excited* and looking forward to trying new recipes, exploring the breadth of vegan food offerings, helping animals, and making positive life changes will have a much easier time transitioning than a newbie vegan who dreads the thought of never eating a steak again. There's some delicious vegan steak out there, but that newbie vegan may not like it or may never try it because they can't get over the notion that cows are delicious and vegans only eat vegetables. The difference lies only in the mindset of these two newbie vegans. One is embracing the changes with eager open arms and an open mind, and the other is focused only on what they've "sacrificed" by switching to veganism. The latter newbie vegan has no incentive to stick with it and probably won't.

The willpower battle is a brutal one, and even the most disciplined willpower warriors often give in to temptation eventually. It's quite a feat for a person to abstain from the things in life that bring them joy. This is why a shift in mindset is so important. For many vegans, continuing to refrain from eating meat and animal products requires absolutely no willpower whatsoever. Some vegans have never once considered that going and staying vegan is difficult, and they may even laugh heartily at the notion. Many who have adopted the ethical vegan lifestyle no longer view meat, dairy, and eggs as food. It takes no more willpower for them to refrain from eating a steak than it does for them to refrain from gnawing on old shoe leather or a piece of dry cardboard.

When first shifting to veganism, it may seem different from the food and lifestyle we're used to, but the longer a person sticks with it, the more it becomes second nature. Many vegans who have been living the lifestyle for a couple years don't find it to be any more difficult than their former meat eating diet and lifestyle. By that point, they've reaped the benefits of improved health and the exciting and varied diet provided by the seemingly endless plant foods the world has to offer. Even after several years of following a vegan diet, many people still enjoy new and exciting plant-based foods on a regular basis. With countless recipes and new vegan products hitting the market constantly, there's always so much to look forward to. It becomes increasingly more difficult to look backward and miss the animal-derived "foods" we used to eat. Many long-term vegans hardly even remember what meat, cheese, or eggs taste like. How can you miss something if you don't remember what it tastes like?

To truly embrace transitioning to a vegan lifestyle without becoming a willpower warrior, focus on the myriad of benefits ahead of you: improved health and energy, possible fat loss, increased fiber intake, decreased environmental impact, decreased global water consumption and water pollution, fun and exciting new foods, vegfests and other vegan events, new friends with a strong common bond, and the peace of mind that you are no longer contributing to animal cruelty and violence. Don't focus on giving up your favorite foods! As we'll soon discover, you don't need to give them up anyway.

Favorite Foods (Non-Vegan)

The number one reason people do not go vegan is taste. People don't want to give up their favorite foods, or more specifically, the taste of their favorite foods. For many people, going vegan not only means change, it means sacrificing all their favorite foods. But what if you could go vegan without giving up any of your favorite foods?

What do you eat? What are your favorite animal-based foods? You may want to pull out a pen and a sheet of paper and write down all the non-vegan foods you enjoy, all the things you believe you'd be giving up if you were to go vegan. Your list might look something like this:

- Steak
- Bacon
- Cheeseburgers
- Meatballs
- Fried Chicken
- Chicken Wings
- Chicken Parmesan
- Pizza
- Milkshakes
- Cheese
- Sausage
- Scrambled Eggs
- Pork Chops
- Ice Cream
- Chocolate
- Mozzarella Sticks
- Tuna Salad
- Breaded Fish Sticks
- Seafood

The good news is that all these foods, and anything else you may have written on your list now come in vegan versions. In addition, many of the vegan versions are almost entirely indistinguishable from the animal-based versions we're so used to. Everything is vegan now! If for some reason, you're unable to find the vegan versions of your favorite foods, many of them can be made easily and cheaply by following a good recipe.

If the number one reason people cite for not going vegan is taste, and the taste of those foods can easily be replicated using plants foods, what then is stopping people from going vegan?

We'll get back to your favorite non-vegan foods soon, but for now let's take a look at your favorite foods that are vegan.

Favorite Foods (Vegan)

Those who say they could never go vegan may not realize they're already about half of the way there. Do you know anyone who eats *only* meat, dairy, eggs, and honey? Nope. Most people eat many plant foods already.

Now flip over the sheet of paper with your favorite non-vegan foods, and on the other side write a list of your favorite foods that are entirely plant-based. The list may look like this:

- Apples
- Oranges
- Grapes
- Watermelon
- Zucchini
- Yellow Squash

- Cauliflower
- Baked Potatoes
- Sweet Potatoes
- French Fries
- Oatmeal
- Pasta
- Hummus
- Peanuts
- Peanut Butter
- Black Beans
- Chickpeas
- Lentils
- Peas

People who eat meat, dairy, and eggs don't *only* eat meat, dairy, and eggs. Chances are that their diet already consists of many vegan foods. One of the easiest ways to transition to a vegan diet is to begin by focusing on all the plant foods you already love and incorporate as many of those into your diet as possible. If you're trying to give up your favorite non-vegan foods, replacing them with the *vegan* foods you love will make the process much easier.

If you focus on the plant foods you love and continue to explore and find new plant foods, you'll be less likely to feel deprived. It's much tougher for anyone to give up *all* of their favorite foods than it is to give up one or two of their favorite foods. The problem is that most non-vegans tend to think of "vegan food" as tofu, lettuce, and more tofu—they forget about the wide variety of plant-based foods they already enjoy. They don't know how easy it can be to make all their favorite foods out of plants instead of animals.

Use this list of your favorite vegan foods to help you decide what to buy the next time you go grocery shopping. You'll eliminate most of the guesswork by already knowing about half of what you're going to eat on a given day.

What to Buy

Before we go any further, please remember one important thing: WHEN TRANSITIONING TO A VEGAN DIET YOU DO NOT HAVE TO GIVE UP YOUR FAVORITE FOODS. Everything is vegan now, including all your favorite foods. While the vegan versions of some of these foods may not taste *exactly* like the versions you're used to, it's only a matter of adjusting to the slightly different flavors. Many new vegans claim they do not like the taste of vegan cheese. But is it the taste of the vegan cheese they don't like…or simply the fact that the vegan cheese doesn't taste *exactly* like the animal cheese they know so well? For many people trying new vegan foods for the first time, the problem

11

isn't necessarily that they don't like the taste. The problem is that some of the vegan foods taste *different*. Any change in diet takes time to adjust. Some vegans who used to *love* animal cheese can no longer tolerate the smell of it after they've been vegan for some time and they've gotten used to vegan cheese. Our tastes change over time and often all it takes is going without the foods we once loved for a few weeks for our taste buds to readjust. Then foods we once loved now smell and taste unappealing.

The vegan versions of some other foods taste virtually indistinguishable from their animal-based counterparts. A few examples of vegan foods that taste the same or better are certain brands of butter, mayonnaise, milk, yogurt, cheese, cheesecake, ice cream, meatballs, sausage, and hamburger. These days there are so many different brands and varieties of vegan food, it's easy to find something you'll like as much as the animal-based versions.

Going vegan is not about depriving yourself. Quite the opposite, in fact. If you're transitioning to a vegan diet and find yourself feeling deprived of your favorite foods, remember that you can still eat all of them! Next time you go grocery shopping, bring the list you wrote earlier of the foods you love that are plant-based, and also scope out what vegan replacement foods the supermarket offers. Grab a few of them and remember to try out different items on your next visit to the supermarket. With a little guess-and-check, you'll find which vegan foods you like and which ones you don't.

Let's get started by exploring your favorite non-vegan foods, and how to replace them with vegan versions that you'll love.

Meat

The meat available for purchase in most developed nations generally comes from the same few animals. Animals such as cows, pigs, chickens, turkeys, fish and crustaceans are regarded as food animals, while the majority of other animals are not. Animals that are considered food will differ depending on the nation, region, and culture, but most people purchasing meat in a developed nation will purchase the meat of one of the animals above. These are the most widely available meats, and therefore are the most common meats to have been veganized.

Vegan food company Gardein offers a line of realistic-looking meatless meat products. Gardein products are found in the frozen section of the supermarket and consist of entirely vegan versions of ground beef crumbles, meatballs, meatloaf, chicken tenders, chicken nuggets, barbeque chicken wings, turkey cutlets, chicken patties, chicken sliders, beef tips, chicken strips, pork bites, beef burgers, breaded fish fillets, and crab cakes. They also offer black bean burgers, breakfast sausage patties, pizza pockets, breakfast scramble pockets, pulled pork pockets, various skillet meals, and more. Gardein products taste practically identical to their animal-derived counterparts and have grown in popularity over the years. Gardein products are now available across the United States and Canada, soon to expand into the United Kingdom and beyond.

Turtle Island Foods offers a line of fully vegan meats under the brand name Tofurky. Their meats are usually made from wheat gluten or soy and are high in protein. Tofurky offers various sausages, deli "meat" slices, roasts and other products. Tofurky products are often found near the tofu in the produce section of the supermarket.

Field Roast offers various sausages, roasts, burgers, and deli slices. Field Roast products are also usually located near the tofu in the produce department of many supermarkets.

A company called Sweet Earth makes vegan bacon, ham and other deli slices, burgers, burritos, frozen curry and stir fry dishes, and has recently launched a line of frozen pizzas.

Lightlife makes vegan burgers, hot dogs, sausages, deli meats, chicken products, and tempeh.

Boca produces a line of frozen vegetarian and vegan burgers, chicken patties, chicken nuggets, and crumbles similar to ground beef.

Chicago food company Upton's Naturals makes a line of vegan meat using seitan and jackfruit. They also offer curry dishes, Thai style dishes, mac and cheese, and burgers. They can be easily recognized by the illustrated portrait of a man in a suit and bow tie on the front of the package whose facial hair changes with each item.

Morningstar Farms offers a wide variety of vegetarian and vegan meats from chicken nuggets to bacon strips. The company recently announced their intent to phase out their vegetarian products and make only vegan food products.

Supermarket chains are catching on to the growth of veganism and many are now offering their own line of vegan foods. International grocery chain Aldi now offers their own line of vegan meats, cheeses, veggie burgers, and other items. Several national and regional supermarket chains such as Trader Joe's and Stop & Shop are also offering their own line of vegan products. As the demand for vegan food continues to grow, more supermarkets will recognize the potential and begin to offer their own line of vegan products.

This is only a partial sampling of the vast array of meat alternatives available. Many smaller vegan food businesses are opening and producing plant-based meats and cheeses that are sold locally. As the demand for plant-based food grows, more vegan food companies will open and bring more offerings to the table. With the vast selection of vegan meats available, you're sure to find something you love as much, if not more than your favorite animal products.

If your access to such vegan meats is limited, there are many ways to make your own vegan meats or meat replacements at home using more accessible and readily available foods. If you have access to textured vegetable protein (TVP), also known as textured soy protein, you can use it as meat in many dishes. TVP is relatively flavorless, and, like tofu, it tends to soak up the flavors and juices of whatever you're cooking it with. TVP is inexpensive and extremely versatile. It cooks up similar to ground beef, so it's perfect for things like taco meat, meatballs, or adding to pasta sauce.

Seitan is made from wheat gluten and is high in protein. Once cooked, seitan becomes eerily similar to meat in both appearance and texture. When seasoned appropriately, seitan also tastes incredibly similar to meat. If vegan meat products are not available in your supermarket, or are too expensive, consider making your own from scratch using wheat gluten. The cost of a bag of wheat gluten is roughly the same as a package of processed seitan sausages, and with the proper ingredients and a few recipes, you can make affordable sausages, steaks, ribs, bacon, and burgers. Seitan is incredibly versatile, and with the right spices and sauces, it's not hard to make seitan look and taste like your favorite meat products. Seitan can be easily cooked in a steamer or rice cooker. It will expand when cooked, so a little goes a long way...making it a filling option for hungry vegans.

If you're unable to find wheat gluten in your local supermarket, try ordering it from Amazon. You may even find a better deal when ordering online. Try not to buy too much until you've had a chance to try a few recipes and decide if you like it. You won't want to shell out a ton of money buying it in bulk only to discover you don't like seitan.

If you're avoiding soy or if you're gluten free, you don't have to rely on TVP and wheat gluten to make meat replacements. Many whole plants foods can be spiced and shaped to look, feel, and taste like meat. With a few good recipes, you can make your own meat from items like lentils, mushrooms, walnuts, black beans, oats, and jackfruit. Many vegan hamburger and meatless meatloaf recipes use basic whole plants foods. They may not taste *exactly* like their animal-derived counterparts, but after giving your taste buds time to adjust to life without animal products, you may enjoy these plant-based meats as much or more than the foods you ate before. By searching the internet and reading a few vegan cookbooks, you'll be able to find excellent recipes for whole foods plant-based versions of the foods you enjoy.

to the animal kingdom, not the plant kingdom. Many people
don't consider the edible portions of these animals to be meat,
but that's exactly what it is. When an animal is killed and
eaten, the parts that are eaten are considered meat.

You don't have to give up seafood when going vegan,
because as with many other non-vegan foods, they can be
veganized. The list of commercially produced vegan seafood
alternatives is growing. In addition to Gardein fishless fillets
and crabless cakes, there are different brands of vegan fish
sticks, crab cakes, shrimp, and fishless tuna.

For those who want to make their own vegan seafood, it's
easy. Seaweed such as nori lends a fishy, seafoody flavor to
various dishes, including sushi. Sushi is easy to veganize since
many varieties of rolls can be made using common sushi
ingredients like cucumber, carrot, mango, and avocado. With
the addition of wasabi, soy sauce, and pickled ginger, you may
think that your vegan sushi tastes the same as the sushi you've
always eaten.

Vegan lobster rolls can be made from hearts of palm,
there's a popular local vegan restaurant that makes crab cakes
out of artichokes, and vegan shrimp can be made from
cauliflower. Many types of vegan fish can be made from

ingredients like tofu, eggplant, or hearts of palm and seaweed. Vegan oysters and clam strips can be made using oyster mushrooms that taste and feel like saltwater oysters and clams. With the addition of vegan tartar sauce and lemon juice, you can still enjoy your favorite seafood dishes as a vegan, and you may even prefer your "fish" without that fishy taste.

Clam chowder can be made vegan by using shiitake mushrooms instead of clams. You can also use button mushrooms or oyster mushrooms. Plant milk and vegan butter work well together to make the creamy base of the chowder. If you don't have mushrooms, you can make corn chowder following a vegan clam chowder recipe and it will taste quite similar.

Tuna salad can be made using vegan tuna produced by Loma or Sophie's Kitchen. If you don't have vegan tuna, canned chickpeas make a wonderful substitute. Once drained and mashed, chickpeas taste like tuna, especially when incorporating a sheet of finely chopped nori seaweed. Add a little vegan mayonnaise (or tahini), a squeeze of lemon juice, and a sprinkle or two of nutritional yeast, and you'll wonder why you've never made tuna salad from mashed chickpeas before.

If you're a fan of caviar, guess what? Caviar can be made vegan as well. Vegan caviar is often made from red or black quinoa, tapioca, or lentils. When seasoned with soy sauce, rice wine vinegar, sesame oil, and nori seaweed, vegan caviar can taste much better than traditional fish egg caviar.

Cheese

Can you guess the number one reason many vegetarians won't go vegan? If you guessed cheese, you're absolutely right. Not only is the salty, fatty flavor of cheese hard for most people to turn away from, but when casein is digested by the human body, it turns into the opioid peptide casomorphin, which produces a morphine-like effect within the body. The taste and mouthfeel of cheese is enough for some people to have trouble saying no, but when taking the casomorphins into account, it's no wonder cheese is practically a legitimate addiction for many people.

Fortunately there are lots of vegan cheeses available on the market these days, and while they may not contain opioids to hook you in quite the same way animal cheese does, the taste and mouthfeel of vegan cheeses are similar to the taste and mouthfeel off animal cheese.

One thing to keep in mind is that if you're used to animal-based cheese, the taste of vegan cheese may seem different or unappealing by comparison. Try completely getting off animal cheese for a few weeks before you begin to taste test different vegan cheeses. You need to give your taste buds some time to reset before trying certain new foods. Similarly, someone who is used to eating lots of sugary foods such as cookies, candies, cakes, donuts, cupcakes, and ice cream may find fresh fruit to be bland and unappealing. However, if that person devotes some time to staying away from the sugary foods, it will give their taste buds time to reset. After a few weeks without any sweets, fresh fruit will taste sweet and delicious again. Vegan cheese doesn't necessarily taste any better or worse than animal cheese, it's just different.

Daiya is a popular vegan cheese company that has branched out and now offers many different vegan products. Daiya makes cheese slices, shredded cheese, cream cheese, macaroni and cheese, creamy salad dressings, yogurt, frozen cheesecakes, and frozen pizzas. They've recently launched ice cream products and frozen cheesy burritos. Their product line is ever-expanding as they continue to offer new and innovative vegan foods.

Another growing and expanding vegan cheese company is Follow Your Heart. Follow Your Heart makes Vegenaise and various vegan cheeses in both slices and shreds. They now make parmesan cheese, salad dressings, yogurt, and the product VeganEgg.

Field Roast produces a line of vegan cheeses called Chao. Chao cheese has quickly become a favorite among vegans, and they now offer a macaroni and cheese dish called Mac 'n Chao. With the popularity of their Chao cheese product line, expect to see more cheese products by Field Roast in the near future.

The vegan cheese company Miyoko's produces an assortment of products, including various cheese wheels, butter, mozzarella, cream cheese, and cheesy spreads. Miyoko's is another company that is growing in popularity, so expect to see new and exciting things from them.

Violife is a vegan cheese company based in Greece. Violife produces cheese in various forms, such as shredded cheese, cream cheese, blocks, and slices. The company distributes their products throughout many European countries and has expanded into the United States.

Kite Hill offers a line of vegan dairy products including ricotta, cream cheese spreads, and cheesy foods such as ravioli and tortellini.

Aldi now offers its own vegan mozzarella shreds and cream cheese under the brand Earth Grown, and as their vegan product line grows, we're likely to see more varieties of vegan cheese.

As with the meats, there are many small businesses popping up that offer vegan cheeses. One such local cheese company that has quickly grown in popularity in recent years is Three Girls Vegan Creamery, based in Connecticut, US.

What began as a small wholesale vegan cheese company has outgrown at least two locations and now operates a popular local eatery that ships their unique line of vegan cheeses, sauces, and meats across the United States. As the demand for vegan products grows, the number of such vegan food companies will continue to increase.

If your access to vegan cheeses is limited, try making your own. A quick search of vegan cheese recipes on the internet will produce a long list of various vegan cheese options. Many of the hard vegan cheeses use cashews, spices, and agar agar powder. However, if you don't have the time to follow a vegan cheese recipe, all you need to create a cheesy flavor is salt, nutritional yeast, and a form of fat, such as cashews or vegetable oil. Nutritional yeast is deactivated yeast that is made from a certain type of sugar-eating fungus, and is completely vegan. It has a cheesy, nutty flavor, and combined with salt and fats such as nuts or vegetable oil, it tastes like cheese. The addition of salt and fats are optional, as nutritional yeast tastes somewhat like cheese on its own. Sprinkling a generous amount on pasta and other foods lends a flavor similar to parmesan cheese.

Milk

Humans are the only species on the planet to make a habit of consuming the milk of another species. We're also the only species on the planet to consume milk past infancy. Humans are highly adaptable creatures, and people likely began consuming the milk of livestock animals thousands of years ago in order to survive times of famine.

Why do we continue to drink cow's milk?

Cow's milk has long been touted (chiefly by the dairy industry itself) as being a healthy form of protein and calcium, however, more recent studies suggest otherwise. The China Study, a book by T. Colin Campbell, Ph.D., and Thomas M. Campbell II, M.D., focuses on a 20 year study of the link between various chronic illnesses and the consumption of animal products. The study found a strong link between the consumption of cow's milk and the increased risk of health problems such as atherosclerosis, cancer, diabetes, osteoporosis, kidney stones, migraine headaches, acne, and obesity.

Long marketed as nature's perfect food—delicious, nutritious, and packed with protein and calcium—in more recent years, cow's milk is gradually being exposed as little more than an unnecessary and potentially harmful product, pushed onto the population by clever marketing campaigns.

Whether you're choosing to remove cow's milk from your diet due to health concerns or due to the appalling treatment of animals inherent in the dairy industry, you'll find plenty of plant milks to choose from instead. The following is a list of some of the more common plant milks. With so many types of plant milk, you're bound to find at least one or two that you like.

- Almond milk
- Cashew milk
- Coconut milk
- Flax milk
- Hemp milk
- Rice milk
- Oat milk
- Soy milk

If none of these milks are available where you shop, you can make your own with a blender, cheesecloth, water, and the source plant food of your choice. Making your own plant milk is quite cheap and easy. Recipes for specific plant milks can be found online.

If you don't have access to any commercially available plant milks or the means in which to make your own, for many recipes you may be able to substitute plain water. Baked items such as muffins, cookies, donuts, and cakes can easily be made with plain water instead of milk. It may alter the taste to some degree, but with different combinations of sweeteners, vanilla extract, and vegetable oil, you may not miss the milk.

Yogurt

Non-dairy yogurt is becoming increasingly more available in the supermarket. Several of the big yogurt companies have even begun to produce non-dairy yogurt to meet the growing demand. Non-dairy yogurt is now available from companies such as So Delicious, Daiya, Silk, Kite Hill, Good Karma, Almond Dream and Coconut Dream, Chobani, Dannon, and Stonyfield. Trader Joe's now makes their own line of non-dairy yogurts as well.

If you're unable to find non-dairy yogurt at your local supermarket you can make your own with a few simple ingredients. With a cup of plant milk, agave nectar or maple syrup, lemon juice, cornstarch, and vanilla extract, you can make your own vegan yogurt anytime. Adding berries and granola is optional. Search for a recipe you like, as non-dairy yogurt recipes can differ greatly.

Butter

A serving of one tablespoon of butter (approximately 14 grams) contains 12 grams of fat, 7 grams of which are saturated fat. Similarly, many vegan butters contain around 10 to 11 grams of fat per tablespoon. No matter how you look at it, butter, whether vegan or not, is almost entirely made of fat. Fat is a flavor that people crave, because along with salty and sweet foods, it means plenty of calories. From an evolutionary standpoint, food that is high in calories is a good thing because it sustains us. Butter is both salty and fatty and is loved by people across the world. The great thing about butter is that the flavor is easy to replicate.

There are many companies that now make vegan butter to fill the growing demand. With so many options in the butter section, you'll want to double-check the ingredients of any buttery spread that doesn't say "vegan" on the package. Earth Balance makes vegan butter in the form of sticks and spreads. Some varieties of Smart Balance are dairy-free, and while they may not say "vegan" on the packaging, double-check the ingredients list to ensure there's nothing animal-derived. I Can't Believe It's Not Butter now makes a vegan buttery spread that says "IT'S VEGAN" in large text on the front of the container. Other companies such as Miyoko's and Melt also make vegan butter, as do a few companies from the United Kingdom, such as Flora, Naturli, and Pure.

Vegetable shortening like Crisco is also plant-based, though not certified vegan. Once again, double-check the label to be sure.

If you're unable to find prepared, packaged vegan butter at your supermarket, why not make your own? There are plenty of easy recipes that you can use to make firm, spreadable vegan butter, but if you don't have the time, all you need to mimic the flavor is a bit of coconut oil and salt. If you don't have coconut oil, any vegetable oil will work. Vegetable oil may not spread quite like butter but the flavor will be close.

Ice Cream

You love ice cream. Who doesn't? There's no doubt that when people first contemplate the idea of going vegan, one of the first things they envision is living a boring, meaningless life without ice cream. Whenever you hear someone say "We all have to die some time. Why not live a little until then?" you know they're talking about ice cream. Ice cream is practically everyone's favorite dessert and I wouldn't blame them for not wanting to live without it. The great news is that no one needs to!

A few short years ago, vegan ice cream options were sparse, with little more than Rice Dream to be found. Not anymore.

There are so many different brands and flavors of dairy-free ice cream these days. You'll gain at least 20 pounds trying them all. Dairy-free vegan ice cream is completely indistinguishable from dairy ice cream in terms of flavor. Practically the only difference to be found is that some brands of vegan ice cream are *slightly* more expensive than dairy ice cream. Another difference for many people who struggle to digest dairy is that vegan ice cream isn't likely to give them stomach cramps and flatulence, as reported by many people who consume dairy.

With so many flavors of vegan ice cream, you won't miss dairy ice cream. In fact, in a blind taste test, you'd never be able to tell the difference. Non-dairy vegan ice cream is so delicious, there's even a vegan ice cream company called So Delicious. There are many different brands of non-dairy ice cream, with more arriving in stores all the time. Non-dairy ice cream is typically made of almond milk, cashew milk, oat milk, rice milk, soy milk, or coconut milk. Each type has its own unique flavors. Almond milk, oat milk, and rice milk ice cream has a milder flavor, while ice cream made from cashew milk, soy milk, and coconut milk taste like cashews, soy, and coconut. Almond milk ice cream is very mild, whether you like almonds or not, you may not be able to taste them in almond milk ice cream. If you're trying non-dairy ice cream for the first time, unless you're crazy about coconuts or cashews...try almond milk.

Companies that offer dairy-free vegan ice cream include:

- Ben & Jerry's
- Bryers
- Coconut Bliss
- Double Rainbow
- Dream (Rice, Almond, Soy)
- Häagen-Dazs
- Halo Top
- NadaMoo!
- So Delicous
- Talenti
- Tofutti
- Van Leeuwen

There are also many supermarket chains offering their own line of dairy-free vegan ice cream, such as Whole Foods, Trader Joe's, Target, Aldi, Stop & Shop, Safeway, and Kroger. Some of the above companies also offer ice cream sandwiches and ice cream bars. Magnum has vegan ice cream bars but they don't yet offer pints.

Once again, vegan ice cream tastes no different than dairy ice cream, and if anything, the flavor of plant milk is milder than cow's milk, so you may even prefer vegan ice cream over dairy ice cream. If you're worried you won't find your favorite ice cream flavor in a dairy-free version, you may be surprised. Here's a small sampling of some of the vegan ice cream flavors offered by the companies above:

- Vanilla Bean
- Chocolate
- Cookie Dough
- Mint Chocolate Chip
- Cookies 'N Cream
- Salted Caramel Cluster
- Snickerdoodle
- Dark Chocolate Truffle
- Cappuccino
- Oatmeal Cookie
- Caramel Apple Crumble
- Coconut Macaroon
- Butter Pecan
- Chocolate Fudge Brownie
- Cinnamon Buns
- Coconut Seven Layer Bar
- P.B. & Cookies

- Coconut Caramel
- Peanut Butter Chocolate Fudge
- The Rockiest Road
- Birthday Cake Cookie Dough
- Java Crunch
- Strawberry & Fudge

If you're drooling by the time you finish reading this list, don't worry, everyone does. With vegan ice cream flavors like these available, who could miss dairy ice cream? Some of the vegan ice creams listed above may be a bit more expensive than dairy ice cream, but not by much. Many are about the same price as dairy, and some brands—Häagen-Dazs and Target's brand, Archer Farms—are cheaper than most dairy ice cream. The question is, if you can get your favorite ice cream in the dairy-free version for roughly the same price, why wouldn't you?

If you want to buy ice cream for your family but don't want to buy three or four different pints, look for Breyers non-dairy. Breyers non-dairy ice cream comes in 1.5 quart cartons that typically cost less than a pint of some of the other brands. The catch being that they only have two flavors so far (Vanilla Peanut Butter and Oreo Cookies & Cream), but both flavors are delicious! The only drawback to buying Breyers non-dairy ice cream in the larger 1.5 quart size is struggling not to eat

the entire carton in one sitting, which is easier than you
might think.

Eggs

Can you imagine the first human being who watched a
chicken (or any bird for that matter) lay an egg? Did they say
"Mmmm, I bet that tastes good!"? Did that person cook the
egg, or did they crack it open and slurp it raw like Rocky
Balboa? Either way, does it sound appealing? Humans began
eating bird eggs thousands of years ago. As with the
consumption of animal milk, humans likely began eating bird
eggs to survive times of famine. Eggs are relatively easy to
obtain and provided early humans with a dense source of
calories and protein.

Things have changed and most people in developed
countries no longer face desperate times of famine. These
days, people who can afford to purchase chicken eggs as a
source of food can easily purchase healthier food. You could
buy two pounds of lentils or split peas for the same price as a
dozen eggs at most supermarkets. A carton of twelve chicken
eggs has about 935 calories and 72 grams of protein, but two
pounds of dried lentils or split peas will provide about 3,200
calories and 220 grams of protein when cooked. If humans no

longer need to eat eggs in order to survive times of famine, why do we still eat them?

The answer is tradition, habit, and taste. We are so used to eating chicken eggs most people have never stopped to consider whether we *should* be eating them. Eggs come from a bird's cloaca, which is the single shared opening of a bird's urinary, reproductive, and digestive tracts. The cloaca is the same hole from which a bird releases not only eggs, but also urine and feces.

Fortunately, anyone who likes eating eggs can enjoy the same flavors and the same dishes completely egg-free. Whether you eat eggs for breakfast or use them in recipes as a binder, eggs can be easily replaced with other foods that do not come from a chicken's butt.

For those who like to eat eggs for breakfast, Follow Your Heart makes a product called VeganEgg. The food company JUST, Inc. (formerly Hampton Creek Foods) makes Just Egg, and Orgran offers Vegan Easy Egg. These products all taste different and you may or may not think they taste like eggs.

If you're unable to find these products, or if you've tried them and weren't impressed, tofu can be used to make a scramble that is practically identical to scrambled eggs in both appearance and taste. With a pinch of turmeric, salt, and pepper, tofu can be scrambled up in a frying pan and cooked the same way as eggs. The turmeric gives the tofu scramble a yellow tint, and the salt and pepper lends flavor in the same way as when sprinkled on eggs. However you cook scrambled eggs for breakfast, try cooking tofu scramble the same way. If you like your scrambled eggs with vegetables, salsa, and hot sauce, try making your tofu scramble that way. If you like your scrambled eggs with sausage and cheese, make tofu scramble with vegan sausage and vegan cheese. If you prefer your scrambled eggs plain with a little salt and pepper, do that with the tofu. You may find it's not the flavor of the eggs themselves that you enjoy, but all the additional veggies, meats, cheeses, and condiments you add to the eggs afterward. If your scrambled eggs are more of a vessel for the mixture of other foods and flavors you add, you'll find little difference when using tofu instead of eggs, as tofu tends to take on the flavors of whatever you're cooking it with.

If you're looking to replace eggs as a binder in baked goods, there are many egg replacers to choose from. Bob's Red Mill makes an affordable egg replacer and a single 12 ounce bag is equivalent to about three dozen eggs. There are other commercial egg replacers made by companies like Orgran and Ener-G, but for baking purposes, many regular food staples can replace eggs as a binder. The following items can be used to substitute one egg for use in baked goods:

- Applesauce (1/4 cup)
- Banana (1/2 banana, mashed)

- Peanut butter (3 tablespoons)
- Silken tofu (1/4 cup)
- Plain non-dairy yogurt (1/4 cup)
- Pumpkin or sweet potato (1/4 cup canned or mashed)
- Ground flax (1 tablespoon, plus 3 tablespoons water)
- Chia seeds (1 tablespoon, plus 1/3 cup water)
- Soy protein powder (1 tablespoon, plus 3 tablespoons water)
- Baking powder (1 teaspoon powder, 1 tablespoon vinegar)
- Mashed avocado (1/4 cup)
- Corn starch (2 tablespoons corn starch, 3 tablespoons water)

Different egg substitutes will work better for different baking needs. For sweet baked goods, try applesauce, banana, plain non-dairy yogurt, pumpkin, or sweet potato. Flax eggs (1 tablespoon flax mixed with 3 tablespoons water) are incredibly versatile and will work with both sweet and savory foods. Ground flax is also fairly cheap and therefore may be the most useful and cost-effective option all around.

Mayonnaise

The selection for vegan mayonnaise needs some improvement, but fortunately mayonnaise is easy enough to make vegan, so most vegan mayonnaise on the market tastes almost exactly like regular egg mayonnaise.

Nayonaise, produced by Nasoya Foods, probably tastes the least like mayonnaise. That's not to say that it tastes bad, that depends on your own personal preference, but if you're looking for a vegan mayonnaise that tastes like the regular egg mayonnaise you're used to, Nayonaise is not it.

The vegan and vegetarian food company Follow Your Heart began producing a vegan mayonnaise called Vegenaise in the late 1970's that eventually became the best selling vegan mayonnaise in the United States. Though immensely popular, Vegenaise doesn't exactly taste identical to regular mayonnaise. That's not necessarily a bad thing—many people think Vegenaise is absolutely delicious. Some even prefer it to regular mayonnaise. Follow Your Heart now offers several varieties and flavors of Vegenaise (chipotle, barbecue, roasted garlic, pesto, sriracha), in addition to horseradish sauce and tartar sauce. Availability has grown as well, as Vegenaise can now be found in many supermarkets, most frequently in the dairy aisle or the refrigerated section of the produce department.

JUST, Inc., formerly Hampton Creek, produces the popular vegan mayonnaise Just Mayo. Just Mayo tastes almost identical to regular mayonnaise, depending on which brand of regular mayonnaise you're used to. Some Just Mayo consumers think it tastes better than any regular mayonnaise. Just Mayo can be purchased in 30 ounce containers or smaller squeeze bottles that come in several flavors, such as wasabi, sriracha, chipotle, garlic, and truffle.

Hellmann's (also known as Best Foods in some locations) now makes a vegan version of their popular mayonnaise and it tastes the same as the mayonnaise they've been producing commercially since 1913. The name Hellmann's is synonymous with mayonnaise and so Hellmann's is the brand most consumers know and love. If you're looking for a vegan mayonnaise that tastes exactly like the mayonnaise you've always eaten, Hellmann's Vegan is the way to go. Not to say it's the best vegan mayonnaise on the market, but it's the most familiar.

You can also make your own egg-free mayonnaise at home using only four simple ingredients. All you'll need is a blender, unsweetened soy milk, vegetable oil, vinegar or lemon juice, and salt. You may need to attempt making your own mayonnaise a few times to get it right, as sometimes the mayonnaise will "break" which means it doesn't emulsify. The broken mayonnaise can often be fixed, but if you're unable to salvage it, you may need to start again. Fortunately soy milk and vegetable oil are inexpensive and you probably won't need to use much before you get the hang of making mayonnaise without it breaking.

Honey

There's some debate among vegans as to whether honey is vegan. Some vegans who recognize that honey is not vegan still feel that it's good to consume honey because they believe it aids the bee population.

Honey is the food bees work hard to produce for themselves. A single bee has to visit up to 100 flowers to collect enough nectar to fill its "honey stomach." When the honey stomach is filled, digestive enzymes begin to work to turn the nectar into honey. Bees will then return to the hive and regurgitate the liquid, which is then left to evaporate and thicken. Once the liquid has thickened, the bees seal it over with wax and leave it to be consumed later. Some people may argue that honey is *not* bee vomit, but let's take a closer look. Nectar is consumed by bees, where it goes into one of two stomachs, digestive enzymes begin turning the nectar into honey, the liquid is then regurgitated so that it can thicken and later be used as food for the hive. Something that is consumed, partially digested, and then regurgitated...is that considered vomit?

You decide.

In order to produce a pound of honey, hundreds of bees will have to visit up to 2,000,000 flowers. A single hive can visit up to 500 million flowers[1] each year. Bees work extremely hard to produce honey as food for their hive, and then humans come and take it from them, often replacing the honey with corn syrup. The main ingredient used to produce honey may come from a plant initially, but when bees process the nectar and convert it to honey, it's no longer a plant food. Honey comes from bees, not flowers, and is therefore not vegan. Taking another creature's food or benefitting from their labor is not in line with vegan ethics.

Bee populations are in decline and bees could use some help from humans. For anyone wishing to keep bees, please feel free to do so. Keeping bees and allowing them to pollinate your crops *without* stealing the fruits of their labor— their food—is a true symbiotic relationship. By all means, please keep bees! It will indeed serve to further augment the bee population. They will diligently pollinate your crops as no human or other insect can. There's no need to take their food from them.

There is something known as "drip honey" which is the overflow that is collected from a bee hive. This is honey that has overflowed out of a hive because the hive is already brimming with honey. There's *probably* nothing unethical about collecting the drip honey, as it will otherwise go to waste, however…why would anyone want to eat bee vomit?

There are plenty of other natural sweeteners that are vegan, affordable, and readily available. Depending on what you were previously using honey for, you may want to have more than one of these honey substitutes on hand to ensure that what you're using will most closely mimic bee honey. The following is a list of some excellent honey replacements.

- Agave nectar
- Blackstrap molasses
- Bee Free Honee
- Brown rice syrup
- Cane sugar (raw)
- Corn syrup
- Date paste
- Maple syrup
- Organic sugar

Agave nectar is popular among vegans as a honey substitute. Agave nectar has a similar taste and consistency to honey, though agave nectar tends to be somewhat thinner and perhaps a little sweeter. Agave nectar can be used as a sweetener in the same way you'd use honey. Try it as a sweetener in tea, oatmeal, and any recipe that calls for honey.

Blackstrap molasses may not always be the best choice to replace honey, but it works well in oatmeal, baked goods, and in many recipes that call for a drizzle of honey. Blackstrap molasses has a unique flavor and is high in iron and calcium. One caveat is that blackstrap molasses will significantly darken everything you add it to.

Bee Free Honee is an apple-based vegan honey alternative made from apple juice, lemon juice, and cane sugar. The flavor is similar to honey and it can be used to replace honey in almost anything.

Brown rice syrup, raw cane sugar, corn syrup, date paste, maple syrup, and plain organic sugar are all excellent substitutes for honey. Each has its own unique flavors and benefits, depending on the recipe you're following. Try using all of them to see which you prefer. Corn syrup, raw cane sugar, and organic sugar are generally the cheapest options and may be best for baking and in situations where a lot of sweetener is required.

To be vegan is to seek to avoid all forms of animal exploitation, and this includes taking food away from bees. With so many delicious vegan sweeteners available, there's no reason to continue using honey. You still have a wide selection of vegan products to sweeten your food with, so please let bees keep the food they worked so hard to produce for their hive. If you want to keep bees to augment bee populations, the bees will be grateful and will reward you by pollinating your crops. That's a true symbiotic relationship and there's nothing unethical about that.

Baked Goods

Muffins, cookies, cakes, pies, donuts, cupcakes, brownies, and banana bread. These are all things you have to give up when you go vegan, right?

Wrong.

All the baked goods you enjoy as a non-vegan you can still enjoy as a vegan. It's true that many commercially available baked goods have eggs, milk, or butter—but these products can easily be veganized. None of the baked goods you enjoy require animal products. Every single one of them can be made using plant milk, egg replacers, vegan butter, vegan margarine, or oil. In fact, some of the baked goods you love can be made without using or replacing these ingredients at all. The animal products in baked goods don't always need to be replaced. In many cases, a simple altering of the combination of ingredients can yield the same or similar results without any specific non-vegan ingredient being replaced by a specific vegan ingredient.

Eggs

Eggs have many uses in baking. They are used to add texture, moisture, and a rich, creamy flavor. Eggs also act as a binder and emulsifier. Depending on the specific use of eggs in a recipe, you may or may not wish to replace them. When using one of the many egg replacers mentioned previously, you may need to experiment to find which replacer works best for you in each recipe. For some recipes, applesauce may do the trick, for others, you may want to use mashed avocado or ground flax mixed with water. Eggs have so many uses in baking, it will take some time to figure out what works. For example, chickpea liquid (also known as aquafaba) can easily be used in place of egg whites to make a vegan meringue.

Milk

The purpose of using milk in baking is to improve moisture, texture, and flavor. Almost any plant milk can be used in place of dairy milk and will yield the same results. Milk is believed to lend a soft, crumbly texture to cakes, which soy milk mimics perfectly, but if you're not picky about having the "perfect" soft crumbly texture in your cakes, any plant milk will do.

Butter

Fat is used in baking to enhance flavor and to help aerate the product during baking to give good texture and volume. Butter made from cow's milk is absolutely not needed for these purposes. Fat is what's important in baking and that fat can come from many other sources, including coconut oil or vegetable oil. If you're using avocado to replace egg, it may even replace (or partially replace) butter, as avocado is an excellent source of fat.

The main ingredients that are needed to create delicious baked goods are flour, sugar, salt, baking powder or yeast, fat, and liquid. Depending on what you're baking, some of these ingredients may not be necessary. Bread may not need sugar, and muffins may not need yeast or salt.

Flour is the main ingredient, and is the base for most baked goods. Sugar is what makes the baked goods sweet. Salt adds flavor to whatever you're baking. Baking powder or yeast is what makes the product rise when baked. Fat adds flavor, moisture, and texture. Liquid turns powdery mixtures into batter that can be poured. As long as you have the basics down, you can make a wide variety of baked goods from the most simple of ingredients.

Flour is a base ingredient and has very little flavor. Baking powder has little flavor. The flavor of milk in baked goods is often overpowered by other flavor-enhancing ingredients, such as sugar and fat. The main flavor enhancing base ingredients used in baking are sugar and fat. As long as you have those and you're using the appropriate amounts of each ingredient, your baked goods will probably turn out quite tasty. For example, if you bake blueberry muffins using flour, sugar, baking powder, blueberries, vegetable oil, and water instead of milk, your blueberry muffins will taste like blueberry muffins. You won't miss the milk, eggs, or salt. If you're baking banana bread and you follow the recipe, but with similar tweaks as with the blueberry muffins, you may not be able to taste any difference between the vegan banana bread and a non-vegan version with eggs and cow's milk.

If you find any of your vegan baked goods lacking flavor, try using other flavor enhancers, such as vanilla extract, cinnamon, or nutmeg. If your baked goods are lacking in fluffiness, try adding a bit more baking powder, or adding unflavored club soda or seltzer water. If the recipe calls for 1 cup of milk, try 3/4 cup (plant) milk and 1/4 cup unflavored seltzer. The bubbles will trap in air, which will make the final product extra fluffy. If you don't have unflavored seltzer, you can use baking soda and water for the same results.

Vegan baking is incredibly easy, but it's different from the baking most people know. Therefore it will take some time and patience to figure out which ingredient mixtures will yield the same results as non-vegan baked goods in terms of flavor, moisture, and texture. Baking is also incredibly forgiving, as long as you don't over-bake and you're using the right ingredients in the appropriate amounts. If something goes afoul and your baked goods don't come out of the oven exactly as expected, you can always dispose of the "failed" baked goods with your stomach and try again. It may take several attempts before you get it right, but as long as the failed attempts taste good, who cares?

Chocolate

Chocolate is made from cocoa beans, which are the seeds of the cacao tree. Chocolate is naturally vegan, however, commercially produced chocolate is generally made by adding milk powder or condensed milk. The addition of cow's milk is not necessary, and commercial dark chocolate can also be sweet and flavorful. Some would argue dark chocolate tastes better than milk chocolate, as the natural flavors of the cocoa haven't been diluted with milk.

There are many brands of dark chocolate produced commercially, and some are sweeter and more flavorful than others. You might have to try a few before you find one that you like best. Try a 56% dark chocolate, as they tend to be sweeter and less bitter. Make sure to double-check the ingredients because some 56% dark chocolate may contain milk solids. If you *must* have milk chocolate, you can. With the growth of veganism, there are now vegan milk chocolates that are available commercially. If you're unable to find any, try making your own. Vegan milk chocolate can be made using cocoa powder, coconut oil, plant milk, sugar, and vanilla extract.

Marshmallows and Jell-O

Foods containing gelatin are not vegan. They're not even vegetarian. Gelatin is a glutinous substance that is produced by boiling water with inedible parts of animals, such as tendons, ligaments, bones, and skin. Gelatin is rather ubiquitous and can be found in many food items you would never suspect. Food additives like gelatin are one reason it's wise to read the list of ingredients on processed foods. Food items that often contain gelatin include:

- Altoids
- Candy Corn
- Cake frosting/icing
- Chewy fruit snacks
- Cheesecake
- Frosted Mini Wheats
- Gum Drops
- Gummy Bears
- Gummy Worms
- Jell-O
- Marshmallows
- Marshmallow Peeps
- Nerds
- Pop-Tarts
- Pudding

- Starbursts
- Throat lozenges
- Yogurt

Some of the items on this list can be produced without gelatin, so it's best to check the ingredients. This is only a partial list. Since gelatin is used in so many foods, there are many food items that are not mentioned here. Once again, gelatin is not suitable for vegans or vegetarians, so be sure to check labels.

Fortunately many of these foods are now made without gelatin. Chewy fruit snacks often contain pectin instead of gelatin, vegan marshmallows are now available, generic Jell-O can be made with agar-agar powder (a substance made from algae), and some toaster pastries (Pop-Tarts) are made without the use of gelatin. While gelatin is used in many foods, it doesn't need to be. Foods with gelatin can easily be veganized, so there's no need to give them up completely.

Coffee

Regular coffee is vegan. Coffee is a beverage made from coffee beans, the seeds of the berries of certain Coffea plants. Similar to chocolate, coffee is naturally vegan until non-vegan ingredients are added to it. If you enjoy your coffee with milk, try adding any variety of plant milk instead. If you're used to adding heavy cream to your coffee, try coconut milk, which is high in fat. If you don't like the taste of coffee with coconut milk, try one of the many commercial vegan coffee creamers made by Silk, So Delicious, Califia Farms, Ripple, Coconut Cloud, or Natural Bliss by Coffee-Mate.

Remember to stay away from non-dairy coffee creamers. Non-dairy creamers usually contain sodium caseinate, a derivative of cow's milk, which means non-dairy coffee creamers are also non-vegan coffee creamers.

Alcohol

Though rarely mentioned on any list of ingredients, many types of beer, wine, and liquor are not vegan friendly. Non-vegan ingredients are sometimes used in the production of certain types of alcohol. Many liqueurs contain dairy, and certain alcoholic beverages use non-vegan ingredients in the production process. Some of the ingredients used are: albumin, casein, charcoal, chitin, coloring, gelatin, glycerol monostearate (can be made from either animal or vegetable fats), honey, isinglass (derived from the swim bladders of fish), lactose, and pepsin.

Alcohol is produced when yeast consumes sugar and excretes ethanol as a waste product. Yeasts are single-celled microorganisms that are classified as members of the fungus family. The natural production of alcoholic beverages is vegan, yet non-vegan ingredients are sometimes used or added as fining agents during the fining process of the production of certain alcoholic beverages.

A simple internet search can inform you as to whether a certain alcoholic beverage is vegan or vegan friendly. The website Barnivore (www.barnivore.com) has lists of various beers, wines, and liquors that are vegan or vegan friendly. Barnivore will also tell you which alcoholic beverages are not vegan. PETA's website also has lists of different beers[2] and wines[3] that are vegan.

If you're unable to find information on whether a particular alcoholic drink is vegan, you can either take the gamble or opt for a different drink. If you take the gamble, you run the risk of possibly later discovering that the swim bladders of fish were used to produce your drink. It may be better to stay on the safe side and stick with beverages you know for certain are vegan.

Protein Powder

Everyone has different protein requirements. These requirements can vary depending on a person's height, weight, activity level, and certain medical conditions. If you feel you're not getting adequate protein from your regular diet, you may want to supplement. Supplementing protein is an easy way to boost your protein levels without having to eat more food or consume many excess calories.

There are a number of different commercial flavored vegan protein powders available. Some of the more popular powders are produced by:

- Garden of Life
- Purely Inspired
- Olly
- Orgain
- PlantFusion
- Sunwarrior
- Vega
- Vivo Life

Each has their own unique flavors and nutrition composition. Many of these also have added ingredients which you may not want. Some of these added ingredients include: natural flavors, xanthan gum, stevia leaf extract, kale powder, alfalfa powder, and many others. Check the labels prior to consuming if you have food allergies or food sensitivity.

Many people choose to use plain, unflavored protein powders, or their own unique blend of protein powders, depending on their goals and protein needs.

- Brown rice protein
- Chia protein
- Hemp protein
- Pea protein
- Pumpkin seed protein
- Soy protein
- Sunflower seed protein

A few of these natural, unflavored protein powders may be harder to find than others, but they can all be purchased online. Two or more protein powders can be mixed in different proportions to create unique blends that will accommodate your protein needs. They each have their own unique flavors and pros and cons. Since they're natural and unflavored, you may prefer the taste of some over others. You may also want to mix them with plant milk or blend them into a smoothie if you find the taste unappealing when mixed with plain water.

Vitamins and Supplements

When you think of your favorite foods, vitamins and supplements may not be the first thing that comes to mind, but they're still an important part of what we eat. Many vitamins and supplements are not vegan due to the fact that they contain ingredients such as gelatin or lanolin.

Fortunately there are many vegan vitamins and supplements available. Check your local GNC or Vitamin Shoppe. Chain stores such as Wal-Mart, Walgreens, and Target may also have the vegan vitamins and supplements you're looking for. Some brands say "vegan" on the container. If you're unable to find them for purchase from a local shop, you should have no trouble finding whatever you're looking for online.

What Else Do You Eat?

What else do you eat? Is there something we haven't covered? There may be exotic meats or endangered species eaten in some parts of the world, but the average person's food comes from markets, supermarkets, and restaurants. If you suddenly find yourself with a hankering for something exotic, like vegan rattlesnake or vegan rat burgers for example, by all means, please be a culinary pioneer and make it yourself! Don't be surprised, however, if other people aren't interested in using the recipe.

In terms of "normal" food, what else are you interested in that we haven't covered? There's a vegan version for practically everything these days, but if whatever you're looking for hasn't already been veganized, why not do it yourself? If it's a popular food, but hasn't been veganized yet, you'll be the one with the goods, and then your friends, both vegan and non-vegan, will hound you to feed them your culinary creations.

Many vegan businesses begin this way. Someone wants to eat a vegan version of their favorite foods, but the vegan versions don't exist (or they do exist, but taste awful), so they create their own. They perfect the method for making that food, share it with others, and before long people ask them to sell their vegan food commercially. Once it is clear there is a demand for their unique vegan products, they create a business centered on their unique creations. Many vegan cheese businesses, vegan meat businesses, and vegan chocolatiers began this way. The demand for vegan food is growing more rapidly than the vegan food supply. The need for vegan food businesses is strong, especially if you have unique and delicious offerings.

Anything and everything you could possibly want to eat can be veganized. So what do you want to see veganized that isn't covered in this book? Whatever you're looking for, try a simple internet search. If you search for "vegan bacon" but you can't find one that looks good to you, try searching for "vegan bacon recipes" instead. These three simple words may be the most useful tool in your toolbox when transitioning to a vegan diet: "vegan ____ recipes". Searching the internet for these three simple words will yield multiple results, and then you can scroll through them and choose whichever looks most appealing.

Frequently buying prepared, processed, packaged vegan food can get pricey over time, but if you're cooking your own versions of these same foods, you can save wads of cash. Buying a four pack of vegan cinnamon raisin muffins at the supermarket might cost you $7 or $8 (if you can find them), but for the same $7 or $8 you can buy flour, sugar, baking powder, vegetable oil, raisins, and ground cinnamon. Then you can make a couple dozen vegan cinnamon raisin muffins for the same price. Likewise, a package of vegan sausages might cost $6 from the supermarket, but if you use that money instead to buy wheat gluten, chickpea flour, and spices, you can make multiple batches of vegan sausages.

If you can't find vegan versions of what you're looking for, make your own. You'll pick up valuable cooking skills, save money, eat well, and impress your friends. Anything they can eat, you can eat vegan. You're limited only by your imagination!

Whole Foods Plant-Based

Many vegans don't want their food to taste like or resemble meat. There can be any number of different reasons for this. They don't like the taste of meat and that's part why they went vegan to begin with. Maybe they do like the taste of meat and don't want their vegan food to taste like it because they find it too tempting. Maybe they're worried if they continue eating these "mock meats" it may make it too difficult to stay away from real meat. Other vegans simply want to avoid processed foods.

Whatever your reason is for wanting to avoid processed vegan meats or cheeses, a whole foods plant-based diet can be sustainable, cheap, and delicious. The internet is flooded with whole foods plant-based recipes. If you can't find a recipe that works for you, create your own. Many delicious vegan meals have been created by people with a handful of random ingredients. They figured out how to whip them all together in a way that tastes great. Start with whatever you have in your cabinets and refrigerator. A bag of dried green or yellow split peas can turn into 2-4 healthy, high protein meals. Rice, raisins, and plant milk can become a delicious rice pudding. Lentils and vegetables can easily become a tasty lentil stew. If you learn to be creative, you'll never run out of delicious ideas.

When following a whole foods plant-based diet, since you do not *need* meat, milk, cheese, or eggs, you do not *need* to replace these things with vegan versions. Whole foods plant-based is about getting down to the nitty gritty, the nuts and bolts of veganism: grains, beans, legumes, nuts, seeds, fruits, and vegetables. With some planning and basic cooking skills, a whole foods vegan diet can be cheap, easy, sustainable, nutritious, and delicious.

One Thing to Remember

When you're transitioning to a vegan diet, it can take a few weeks for your taste buds to adjust. When you first try vegan versions of your favorite foods, you may find that some of them don't taste *exactly* like the foods you're used to.

It could be that you haven't given your taste buds enough time to adjust. If you're used to cow cheese pizza and have it one night, then the very next night you have your first vegan cheese pizza, you may not like it as much. It's not necessarily that the vegan cheese pizza tastes bad, but you're used to the cow cheese pizza and the vegan one tastes different. If you're a picky eater seldom open to trying new foods, you may need to lay off the cow cheese pizza for a few weeks before trying the vegan version.

It could be that the first vegan pizza you try simply isn't a very good pizza. Some pizza tastes better than others, vegan or not. If you don't enjoy your first vegan pizza, maybe you bought one without much flavor, or with low quality ingredients. That doesn't mean you should write off all vegan pizza forever. The next one you try might be one you thoroughly enjoy. Have you ever had a non-vegan cheese and meat pizza you did not like? How does that compare to the pizza from your favorite pizza place? As there is some bad non-vegan food out there, there is also some bad vegan food out there. Not every vegan food item is going to taste good to every person. Try different things and different variations of the same foods. Eventually you will find something you like as much, if not *more* than your favorite non-vegan foods.

Do all the vegan versions of the foods you enjoy have to taste *exactly* like the original? Some vegan foods will taste different. That doesn't mean they can't be a delicious replacement that you'll be happy with. Take vegan cheese for example. If you absolutely love Chao cheese and could eat it every single day…does it really matter if it doesn't taste identical to cow cheese? Can it still be a viable replacement food for you on your vegan diet? If you like it about 95% as much as the cow cheese you've grown to love, is that 5% too much of a sacrifice?

Going vegan is not about depriving yourself. Going vegan is not about giving up your favorite foods. Going vegan is the exact opposite—it's about opening doors to all the new and exciting food out there that you've been missing out on while eating the same basic cuts of meat, the same basic cheeses, the same basic meals. If you're willing to taste-test and experiment with different recipes, you'll find all the food you could ever desire on a vegan diet, and then some. Going vegan is not difficult or restrictive. Eating the same few animals and the same few products derived from those animals is restrictive. A pig gives only one flavor of bacon, but with vegan bacon, the varieties are limitless!

The more you see how little you have to lose by going vegan and how much you stand to gain, the easier the transition will be for you.

Are you ready?

Before You Transition

Now that you know you can transition to a vegan diet without giving up your favorite foods, let's get ready to make the switch. Before you begin your transition, the first thing you'll want to do is make a basic plan. Your plan can be written or in your head, it doesn't matter. Your plan can include: how long your transition will take, a clearly defined timeframe for how long you're going to stay vegan before you assess how it feels and if you'll stick with it, a list of items to pick up at the grocery store, a list of easy meals you can use to get you through your first few weeks, a list of ingredients to avoid, a few good websites or cookbooks to use for recipes and inspiration, a vegan friend or two you can turn to for tips or advice...and anything else you think will help make your transition easy and fun.

Know your weaknesses. You may want to have a list of vegan foods you can buy in case you get a strong craving for something in particular. You don't necessarily have to purchase that food, only to know where you can get it. If you're addicted to macaroni and cheese, for example, and you worry you won't be able to stay vegan for long because you can't live without it, make sure you know where you can get a good vegan macaroni and cheese. For example, Daiya makes a delicious traditional mac and cheese that is now available in many supermarkets and in most Target stores. If you know your weaknesses in terms of food, you'll be better prepared to handle cravings as they occur.

Figure out what you can eat in a pinch. Let's say your car breaks down in front of a McDonald's. You're waiting for a tow truck. It's been an hour but no sign yet. You haven't eaten breakfast and you're famished. You're tempted to run in for a Big Mac and fries. You figure you've only been vegan for a week and it wouldn't be too tough to reset the clock and start over again at Day One tomorrow or the next day when your car is fixed and your hunger isn't making the decisions for you. Then you remember you have a few Cliff bars and a bag of trail mix in the back seat in case of an emergency. Things come up. Instead of letting any of those things become a reason for you to cheat, be prepared for them ahead of time.

Tell people you're going vegan. Tell at least a few friends and family members about your plan to transition to a vegan diet, and tell them how long your vegan trial period will be. Not only will it give you some level of accountability (you'll be more likely to stick with it in order to remain true to your word), but you also may pique their interest in transitioning to a vegan diet as well. They may even want to join you. If you have a friend or two who are going vegan with you, it'll be like having a spotter at the gym. You can inspire each other, share ideas and recipes, go out to eat together and discuss the changes in your lives and the challenges you're facing.

The more carefully thought-out your plan is, the easier it will be to stick with it, especially during times when you're hungry and you don't have anything readily available to eat.

Reading Labels

There's a funny meme floating around on the internet that depicts a head of broccoli. There are four pictures of the same head of broccoli in the meme, each picture zooming closer to the broccoli. There's clearly text written directly on the broccoli stalk, and as we zoom in closer via the four pictures, on the last one, a close-up of the text shows that it reads: "Ingredients: Broccoli, Milk Powder (1%)".

The meaning of this meme might be lost on newbie vegans, but anyone who has been following a vegan diet for a while will understand. Animal byproducts and their derivatives are ubiquitous in food production. You can find them in countless foods that would otherwise never contain animal ingredients. For additional frustration, the added ingredients don't seem necessary—they could have easily been omitted without altering the taste, nutrition, or shelf-life of the food.

Nutri-Grain bars and other fruity cereal bars often contain whey, many commercially produced breads and bagels contain milk, honey, or L-cysteine, vegetable and herb boxed stuffing often contains chicken broth, certain brands of salsa contain Worcestershire sauce (which contains anchovies), some frozen French fries contain beef tallow, some types of pasta contain eggs, dark chocolate may have milk fat or milk solids, non-dairy creamer contains sodium caseinate, baked beans may have bacon or honey, marshmallows and Pop-Tarts contain gelatin, and refried beans are often made with lard.

This is a small sampling of the many foods that may otherwise be naturally vegan except for the animal byproducts added for no apparent reason. Imagine for a moment buying a box of vegetable and herb stuffing only to smell something funky when you cook it. You retrieve the box from the recycling bin and discover that the funky smell is chicken broth. What do you do with the stuffing? You can give it to someone you know who eats meat, but otherwise you'll probably end up throwing it in the trash. What a waste! Why is there chicken broth in vegetable and herb stuffing? Maybe you buy a bag of frozen French fries only to learn later that there's beef tallow in them. Let's hope you didn't eat any of them before making the discovery. French fries are peeled and cut potatoes, why would anyone add beef tallow to them? The world will never know.

Unfortunately this type of thing is quite common. Hence the meme with the list of ingredients on a simple stalk of broccoli: Broccoli, Milk Powder (1%). That's not to say broccoli truly contains milk protein—it's just a joke—but it's a joke based on truths that vegans must face every day when reading the ingredients lists of the food they buy. From "veggie" burgers that have eggs or cow cheese, to curry paste containing shrimp, you never know what non-vegan ingredients may be lurking in your otherwise vegan food. Especially when the animal byproduct is listed as "2% or less of the following" on the label. It begs the question: why add it to begin with?

This is why it's so important for vegans to read labels carefully. In a world dominated by chopped up animals and products derived from those animals, you never know what might end up in your "vegan" food. Certain processed food items that are vegan from one brand may be made with non-vegan ingredients by another brand. It could be the same food, same flavor, and the same ingredients except for one or two. Some food companies (especially Aldi brands) may even alter their ingredients periodically, so that food that may have once been vegan now contains non-vegan ingredients. The packaging and nutrition information may be the same. The only thing to have changed is one or two ingredients. If you've been buying a certain food product for some time and suddenly the ingredients change, you won't necessarily know. If you make a habit of reading labels, even periodically checking the labels of foods you already buy regularly, you'll be able to avoid unwittingly ingesting non-vegan food.

If you want to avoid having to read labels constantly, consider a vegan diet with minimal processed foods. Heavily processed foods often have a *loooong* list of ingredients, and many of those ingredients can be difficult to identify without a degree in chemistry or food engineering. If you're reading a long list of ingredients and you're unable to identify many of them, there's no way to know whether the product is vegan without researching each ingredient—and even then, certain ingredients can be either animal or plant-derived, so you may still not know. The easiest way to avoid these questionable ingredients is to avoid heavily processed foods, or at least avoid processed foods that have ingredients you can't identify.

Hidden Non-Vegan Ingredients

Don't you love it when you're reading the ingredients of a processed food item and the list is longer than the last novel you read? Assuming the last novel you read was written in Latin, because *who knows* what half of those ingredients are anyway? You may have had straight A's in chemistry and still not know what those ingredients are in your food.

There are so many animal-derived food additives, it would be difficult to cover them all here, but here's a look at some of the more common ones. Some of these items can be derived from either animals or plants, but it's nearly impossible to know which. Any product that carries the "Certified Vegan" label is fine. Otherwise it's safest to avoid these ingredients in general.

- Albumen
- Aspartic acid
- Beeswax
- Calcium carbonate
- Carmine (or cochineal extract)

- Casein
- Collagen
- Confectioner's glaze
- DATEM
- Diglycerides
- Disodium inosinate
- Food grade wax
- Gelatin
- Glycerin
- Keratin
- Isinglass
- L-Cysteine
- Lactic acid
- Lactose
- Lanolin
- Lard
- Lecithin
- Linoleic acid
- Lipids
- Methionine
- Monoglycerides
- Oleic acid
- Pepsin
- Polysorbates
- Rennet

- Shellac
- Sodium caseinate
- Stearic acid
- Tallow
- TBHQ
- Uric acid
- Whey
- Xanthan gum

Once again, some of these ingredients may be derived from plants, but there's no way to know for sure. Highly processed foods aren't healthy to begin with, so you may want to avoid foods that contain these ingredients, regardless of whether they are derived from animals or plants. The list may seem long and impossible to remember, but many of the above ingredients are easy to avoid if you're eating mostly whole foods. As more products are certified vegan, it will become easier to avoid such additives and rest comfortably in the knowledge that if you find any of the above in your certified vegan products, they are plant-based.

Questionable Ingredients

There are other ingredients used in food production which may technically be derived from plants, but the process or processes used to obtain them may not be vegan. In these cases you will need to decide for yourself whether you're willing to purchase and consume foods that contain these ingredients.

Coconuts are vegan but some vegans eschew the consumption of coconuts and coconut products because on certain coconut farms, the fruits are harvested by "worker" monkeys. In some parts of the world, coconut farmers intentionally breed and train monkeys to pick coconuts. It's been reported that many of the monkeys are mistreated by their handlers and the animals are essentially slaves. Coconuts may be vegan but this process of harvesting the fruit is not. It's impossible to know whether the coconuts and coconut products you purchase are from one of these farms, so some vegans (albeit a small minority) choose to avoid coconuts and coconut products altogether.

Palm oil is found in many foods. It's vegan by nature, but the production process is incredibly destructive. Oil palms grow best in tropical climates, so in order to establish palm oil plantations, producers must clear trees in tropical rainforests, predominantly in Indonesia and Malaysia[4]. This process kills many animals, not to mention the effects deforestation has on the environment.

Table sugar is vegan but the refining process is not. Cane sugar is refined in a process that filters it through bone char to achieve the white color. Bone char is what is what it sounds like—charred animal bones—and it is used as a filter in the process of refining cane sugar. Not all white sugar has been filtered though bone char, however, and the process is becoming less common as more cost-effective methods of refining cane sugar are becoming more popular. White sugar that is labeled organic is never processed using bone char.

Vegan food products are occasionally tested on animals. Impossible Foods was reported to have submitted soy leghemoglobin[5] (an ingredient found in their Impossible Burger) to the FDA for testing in order to obtain approval that the ingredient is "generally recognized as safe" (GRAS). Though the company claims there has been no further animal testing in regards to the Impossible Burger, many vegans still refrain from eating the product due to the fact that the ingredient was tested on animals in the past. Similarly, Hampton Creek (now JUST, Inc.) was reported to have submitted mung bean protein to FDA in order to obtain the GRAS recognition. While the company claims no rats were killed to assess digestibility of the mung bean protein, animal testing in and of itself is not considered vegan, and generally once all testing is completed, the subject animals are euthanized. These products may indeed be vegan, but the controversy continues as to whether it is considered acceptable for vegans to consume foods and other products that have been tested on animals.

These examples are only a small sampling of questionable ingredients. Since food production processes are always changing, it's important for anyone who wishes to avoid questionable products and ingredients to keep up to date on what's happening in the vegan world. Even taking all the above into account, adhering to a vegan diet doesn't have to be difficult. Nearly all of these ambiguous and questionable ingredients can be avoided by reading labels vigilantly and choosing whole foods over processed foods whenever possible.

Manufactured in a Facility That Also Processes....

Many foods have this warning on the label, usually somewhere after the list of ingredients. This warning is considered to be almost exclusively for the benefit of those who suffer from allergies, and also to limit the liability of the company that manufactures the product. People with severe food allergies may need to avoid foods with this warning if the warning lists the food item they are allergic to. For example, Vega protein powder includes the warning: "Manufactured in a facility that also processes peanuts, dairy, soy, egg, and tree nuts." Bob's Red Mill hemp protein powder has the warning: "Manufactured in a facility that uses tree nuts, soy, wheat and milk." Many vegan products display similar warnings. The warning is not to suggest that the product actually contains any of those things, it's merely a warning for food allergies.

For people with severe food allergies, in some cases being in the same room with the food item they're allergic to can be enough to cause a reaction—cross contamination does not necessarily need to occur. If you see such a warning on your food, provided you have no allergies to the food items mentioned, there's no need to worry—you can eat products with these warnings and still be a proud vegan.

Staples

A common problem many people face when first transitioning to a vegan diet is that they don't know what to eat. In the United States and many other developed nations, when people think of a plate of food, they envision a large slab of meat, a pile of potatoes, rice, or some other starch, then a small serving of vegetables. When they try to envision a plate of vegan food, they see the pile of potatoes or rice, the small serving of vegetables, and nothing else. They think "Oh man! I'm gonna starve!"

When transitioning to veganism, many people focus only on what's lacking, what's not on their plate anymore, what they've given up. They become so focused on the foods they can't have anymore, they hardly begin to consider that there's countless edible plant foods out there that taste as good as, or better than any animal products. With a little time spent adjusting to their new lifestyle, they'll be able to have their fill of all sorts of delicious food. Instead of seeing a plate with nothing but a pile of potatoes and a few bites of vegetables, thinking they'll starve, why not begin by doubling that pile of potatoes and increasing the serving of vegetables by several times? It may not be the healthiest, most balanced meal, but at least they won't starve. With the immediate problem of imminent starvation averted, newbie vegans can begin to focus on what to put on that plate to take the place of the slab of meat that's no longer there.

Staple foods are foods that are eaten regularly and in quantities that comprise a dominant portion of a person's diet. For many people, this would be meat, dairy, and eggs, often with other foods added in almost as an afterthought. When transitioning to a vegan diet, the staple foods of meat, dairy, and eggs need to be replaced with vegan staple foods — preferably foods that taste good, are affordable, and provide lots of calories and nutrition. If you think of the slab of meat on that plate as the staple food, and the potatoes and veggies as an afterthought, what can you do to veganize that plate and ensure the person eating it will not starve? You can start by replacing the meat with a vegan staple food high in calories and nutrition. How about lentils? With a generous portion of lentils to fill in for the missing meat, how about reducing the serving of potatoes (optional) and then increase that serving of vegetables by several times? Now you've got a protein-packed meal, loaded with nutrition and high in calories. The protein and calories from the lentils combined with the fibrous bulk of the pile of veggies will keep you satiated.

It will help to have a list of staples you love so that at no point in time will you be starving, nor will you be tempted to "cheat" on your "diet" by eating meat or other animal products. Remember not to focus on the missing meat and the half-empty plate. Fill that plate with new, exciting foods that you're not likely to tire of anytime soon. When you do tire of them, there will be more delicious, filling vegan foods to take their place.

The following staple foods are filling, affordable, nutritious, and tasty. If you base the bulk of your diet on these foods, you won't have to spend a fortune and you'll never find yourself feeling hungry after a meal.

- Black beans
- Chickpeas
- Red beans
- Split peas
- Green lentils
- Red lentils
- Oats

- Rice
- Whole grain breads and cereals
- Potatoes
- Sweet potatoes
- Carrots
- Celery
- Frozen vegetables
- Bananas
- Apples
- Tofu

This is only a sample list. Your list may be different. The above foods are nutritious, versatile, filling, and affordable in most places. If you fill your cabinets and refrigerator with foods from this list or staple foods from your own list, you'll always have plenty of food and you'll never have to starve. It's a common misconception that vegan food isn't as filling. That's not true. What is true is that many new or aspiring vegans see vegan food as little more than vegetables and salad. No one will be able to subsist on vegetables and salad alone — there aren't enough calories.

One cup of dry lentils provides 640 calories and 44 grams of protein when cooked. If you add a bag of frozen vegetables to that, you're looking at a meal of approximately 740 calories and 52 grams of protein for about $1.75. That's a filling meal

B . W . L E E T E

indeed, but if it's not enough food for you, try adding more lentils and more veggies. If you're trying to fill up on salad, forget it! You'll spend $20 and you'll be hungry an hour later. This is why it's so important to have a good rotation of staple foods in your kitchen. That way you'll never go hungry and you'll never get bored.

If you don't like these staple foods, what do you like? Make your own list so you won't have to wonder what to put on your plate in place of the meat. Avocado, oranges, corn, quinoa, barley, kidney beans, lima beans, peanuts, peanut butter, raisins, pasta, beets, pears, Textured Vegetable Protein, and seitan. If money's tight you can focus on what's on sale. If money isn't an issue, why not add some Gardein meatballs or beefless grounds to your rotation?

If you make your staples the main focus of your diet, everything else will be easy. You won't have to worry about what you're going to pick up at the supermarket next time you go shopping. You won't have to worry about what you're going to cook for dinner each night. You won't be frantically scouring the internet for recipes. As an omnivorous diet is second nature for anyone who's been eating that way for years, a vegan diet will become second nature in time as long as you realize you don't need to overhaul your diet completely. You can still eat the same food you ate as an omnivore, only veganized.

List of Meals

If you're still worried about what you're going to eat while you're transitioning, put together a short list of meals you love that you can turn to when you're not sure what else to eat. The easiest way to do this is to pick five to seven meals you enjoy that can easily be veganized or that are naturally vegan. If your breakfast is oatmeal with fruit and hemp protein, that's perfect. That's one meal down already. If you enjoy bagels with butter and cream cheese, why not have bagels with hummus instead? That's two meals. If you like hamburgers for dinner, find a great veggie burger recipe that you can make in larger batches and freeze for when you're hungry. Mashed black beans, oats, chopped tomato, and spices combine together well to make a delicious and filling veggie burger once baked in the oven. You can easily and affordably make large batches and freeze them for later. Making your own veggie burgers is cheaper and healthier than buying processed frozen veggie burgers, but if you're pressed for time, you can always fall back on the frozen supermarket burgers.

If you like meatloaf for dinner, try a lentil loaf instead. If you're used to chicken stir fry, try a tofu stir fry. If your meals look like the plate we discussed earlier—large slab of meat with potatoes and a few bites of veggies—try the same meal with seasoned black beans, lentils, or Beyond Burgers in place of the meat.

If you have a list of five to seven vegan meals you love, it will give you time to figure out how to veganize other dishes and discover new recipes. Many people who follow an omnivorous diet consume a wide variety of naturally vegan foods but have never taken the time to consider how to put it all together to live off of those foods alone. Having a good list of vegan staple meals will afford you that time to figure everything else out.

- Oatmeal with fruit and hemp protein
- Whole grain bread with peanut butter and fruit
- Breakfast shake with added plant protein
- Veggie burger on a bagel with lettuce, tomato and hummus
- Lentil loaf with whole wheat pasta, tomato and basil
- Tofu with barbecue sauce, potatoes and vegetables
- Sweet potato and black bean curry with cauliflower over rice

If these meals seem too complicated, you can simplify. Rice and beans with salt and pepper. Pasta, chickpeas, and vegetables all boiled together. Rice, cubed tofu, and vegetables all tossed into the rice cooker. Split peas with salt and pepper. Eating vegan doesn't have to be complicated, even in the beginning when you're trying to figure it all out.

Need dessert? Banana, pineapple, coconut, all mashed and mixed together, then freeze. Now you have nice cream. Or make rice pudding. Drop cooked white rice, plant milk, cinnamon, sweetener, and raisins into a pot and cook until the mixture is pudding consistency. Refrigerate when cool. Too much work? Pick up a pint of Häagen-Dazs coconut milk ice cream.

If you have a list of at least five to seven go-to meals, you can focus on rotating between those while you learn new meals to make. Then if you try one or two new recipes a week, your list will grow. Eventually you'll have a general understanding of what constitutes a healthy, filling, well-rounded vegan meal, and you won't need to follow recipes anymore. You'll know what and how much to cook to keep you satiated, and you'll no longer feel deprived or unsure of what to eat.

When you've amassed a long list of go-to meals, you can decide what new meals to add, or what to take away when you grow tired of something. You can still keep a list of recipes and add to it regularly. Remember, going vegan is not about giving up your favorite foods. Whenever you find yourself with a craving for something you used to eat, instead of sulking and pining for that food, all you have to do is veganize it!

Eating Vegan is Not Expensive

If you've ever heard that following a vegan diet is expensive, forget that. That's a pack of lies. Whoever told you that probably had a myopic view of veganism. Maybe they see vegan food as being organic salads and raw, organic vegetables. With the meager amount of calories in salad and vegetables, you'd probably have to eat $20 worth to be full, and then you'll be hungry again an hour later. Or maybe they see vegan diets as being processed "fake" meat, processed "fake" cheese, and processed "fake" dairy products. Of course that'll be an expensive diet. Processed foods are rarely cheap or filling, whether they are vegan or not. You have to eat a lot of processed "fake" foods to be satiated.

Rice, beans, chickpeas, lentils, oats, pasta, potatoes, sweet potatoes, peas, carrots, celery, corn, bananas, couscous, quinoa, bread, and bagels. Most of these foods are affordable in many parts of the world. Flour is incredibly cheap, and so is sugar and vegetable oil. With a 10 pound bag of flour, a 5 pound bag of sugar, baking powder, cinnamon, vegetable oil, bananas and raisins (about $10-12 total), you can make enough banana bread, cinnamon raisin muffins, and pancakes to feed a small army of vegans. A 10 pound bag of flour will produce about 120 jumbo muffins. The more creative you are with your food, the more affordable it will be to follow a vegan diet.

Meat, dairy, and eggs tend to be the most expensive foods because so much time, energy, money, and resources are required to produce them. In many parts of the world, regular meat consumption is associated with affluence. In Arnold Schwarzenegger's autobiography, *Total Recall*, he discusses how when he was growing up in Austria, his family was very poor and did not frequently eat meat. It wasn't until he joined the Austrian army at age 18 that he began eating meat daily. He was already quite big and strong by then, by the way.

A vegan diet *can* be expensive, as any diet can be expensive. If you don't cook at all, you eat out often, and you try to fill up on salad and raw vegetables all the time, eating vegan will be expensive. Finding balance is the key to making a vegan diet healthy, delicious, and affordable. If you can find a happy equilibrium between the expensive foods and the affordable staple foods, you should be able to create a vegan diet that is healthy, tastes good, and will not drain your bank account.

You'll Learn Mad Cooking Skills

One of the glorious things about being vegan is that it's the perfect opportunity to learn some amazing cooking skills. Vegans are still in the minority and much of the food available at supermarkets and restaurants is not vegan. That means if you want to enjoy certain foods, you need to either find prepared vegan versions of them, or you'll need to learn how to cook.

For example, if you have a strong craving for a blueberry muffin, but are unable to find any vegan muffins for sale at the grocery store, you may have no other choice but to learn to bake vegan blueberry muffins yourself. You scour the internet for blueberry muffin recipes and you find the perfect one. You buy whatever necessary ingredients you don't have already and you get to work. Half an hour later, you pull a fresh batch of blueberry muffins out of the oven. They smell utterly divine. You eat one and marvel in the fact that you have five more you can eat or give to friends. Not only have you learned to bake vegan muffins, but you've avoided a plethora of nasty preservatives and additives that are used to keep store-bought muffins looking and smelling fresh. You've also saved money and now have the ability to make more muffins from the raw ingredients you bought.

The next day you have a hankering for a nice, meaty veggie burger. Unfortunately, the veggie burgers available at the supermarket are frozen, small, and expensive. So you jump back on the internet and do some searching until you find a mouth-watering black bean burger recipe. Once you have all the ingredients, you make a large batch of a dozen large, meaty veggie burgers for less than the cost of buying a box of four frozen patties at the supermarket. Not only have you learned to cook veggie burgers from fresh ingredients, but now you have enough burgers to feed an entire family.

A week later you're invited to a vegan potluck dinner but you have no idea what to bring. You contact a local vegan restaurant that offers catering and you're shocked at the price of a large tray of food. You realize you can make your own for less than half the price, but you've never made that much food before and you don't know what to do. You remember that a friend gave you a cookbook when you first went vegan, and while flipping through it you find a recipe for vegan lasagna that would be perfect. You go shopping for the necessary ingredients and when the day of the potluck comes, you taste-test the lasagna fresh out of the oven. It's one of the best lasagnas you've ever had and you realize you can easily make it again anytime.

The longer you stick with a vegan diet, the more often this will happen. Eventually you'll build a collection of recipes and you'll gain more confidence in your cooking abilities. Not only will you learn to cook meals, but you'll also learn how to make ingredients to use in those meals, such as cheese, sour cream, butter, sausages, stuffing, gravy, pesto sauce, and plant milk.

If you've always loved to cook, going vegan can open up a whole new world of culinary possibilities. If you never had much skill in the kitchen but always wanted to learn, switching to a vegan diet can open up those doors. As a vegan, there are many things you might not find anywhere else and will learn to cook yourself out of necessity—especially if you're craving your favorite foods and have no other way of getting your fix.

For many vegans, the best part of learning to cook is that it often allows them to eat healthier while also saving money. Whether vegan or not, cooking your own food at home is generally much cheaper than buying restaurant food, or prepared, packaged, processed food from the grocery store. If you can't find a recipe for whatever you're looking to make, try your hand at making it from scratch without a recipe. Guess and check. If you make it the first time and it's not perfect, you'll know what to do next time to get it right, or at least make it better. Learning to cook is a useful skill that you may not have developed had your unconventional diet not nudged you in that direction. If you continue to develop your skill by cooking often and by regularly trying out new recipes, you may find yourself in the unique position of being able to turn your new skill into a thriving vegan food business.

Don't Like to Cook?

If you don't like to cook and have no desire to learn, you'll spend a bit more money, but a vegan diet is still totally doable. If you have the money to spare and can afford to eat out more often and buy prepared vegan food from the supermarket, you have lots of options.

Alright, you don't like to "cook" food, but how do you feel about "preparing" food? You don't necessarily need to know how to cook in order to make things like oatmeal, smoothies, sandwiches, salad, chickpea salad, three bean salad, guacamole, Thai spring rolls, vegetable sushi rolls, boxed couscous, tabbouleh, stuffed pita pockets, baked sweet potatoes, peanut butter and jelly, Buddha bowls, and bagels with hummus. Some of these foods may require chopping, mashing, wrapping, or boiling water, but hardly require any actual "cooking."

If you have a crock pot or an instant pot, all you have to do is toss a few items in and press a button or two. Let the machine do the cooking for you. If you have a rice cooker, you can make an entire meal in it similar to a crock pot or an instant pot. Throw in some rice, vegetables, a can of beans or chickpeas, add water, and then all you have to do is hit one button. How could it be any easier than that?

If that's still too much cooking for you, or if all you have is a microwave, there are still many things you can zap in the microwave without having to cook anything. Baked potatoes or sweet potatoes, bean quesadillas, frozen French fries, vegan macaroni and cheese, vegetable "fried" rice, steamed veggies, and mug cakes, to name a few.

If you're completely unwilling to prepare anything at all, don't worry, you can still be vegan without breaking the bank. Most fruit requires no preparation besides cutting or peeling, hummus wraps and other sandwiches like peanut butter and jelly require practically no preparation, canned beans topped with salsa is easy and doesn't require cooking, chips with salsa make for a great snack, and so does raw vegetables and hummus, or peanuts and raisins. If you're willing to be creative, the possibilities are endless.

If this is all *still* too much work, no worries. As long as you're not concerned with the cost of your food, you can focus on prepared microwaveable food like frozen pizzas, Gardein skillet meals, potato and onion pierogies, and meals by Kashi, Sweet Earth, Amy's, Daiya, and Morningstar Farms products that are labeled vegan. There are also vegan meal delivery services by Hungry Root, Epicured, Terra's Kitchen, Green Chef, Urban Remedy, Veestro, and Purple Carrot. Be sure to check their websites to make sure they deliver in your area. Some of these services offer both vegan and vegetarian options, so check their menus ahead of time.

Pre-Transition Grocery Shopping

Now that you have a better understanding of how fun, easy, and affordable transitioning to a vegan diet can be, it's time to start the transition. You know you will not have to give up all your favorite foods. You know what you can buy or cook to replace all the things you love. You have a rough plan for how to begin your transition. The hard part is over. The next thing you need to do is stock up on food.

This book is about transitioning to a vegan diet and lifestyle, not continuing on with an omnivorous or vegetarian diet. Therefore we won't focus on purchasing any further animal products. If you feel the need to buy more animal products as you transition, that's your call, but we won't be discussing it here. Your pre-transition grocery shopping list should be entirely vegan because your goal is to transition to being entirely vegan, and if you act according to your goal, the process will be easier. Purchasing meat, dairy, or eggs during your transition only sets you up for failure. If it's there in your kitchen, staring you in the face, it'll be too tempting to avoid. Then if you do it eat it, the next time you go grocery shopping, it will be all the more tempting to buy more meat, dairy, and eggs. If you align your actions with your intent by buying only vegan food, you set yourself up for success from the start.

To get started on your grocery list, revisit your list of favorite vegan foods from earlier in the book. How many of those are staple foods? If you stock up on a few of the staple foods you love—let's say lentils, beans, oats, and rice—then add some fruits, vegetables, nuts and seeds, you'll have a strong list of the foods which will make up the bulk of your diet for the next week or so. Then add some vegan meats, vegan cheeses, and dessert foods if you have a sweet tooth.

Most supermarkets will have all these items, so you can shop around to find the good sales. Since you may not be used to buying some of these items, you may have to explore the supermarket a bit to find what you're looking for. Certain vegan food items will not be where you expect them to be. Some veggie burgers will be in the produce aisle near the tofu, and others will be in the frozen foods section. Some supermarkets may have non-dairy ice cream in the same aisle with the regular dairy ice cream, and others may keep it in a "Natural Foods" section. If you're looking for Beyond Burgers, don't look in the frozen foods section with the other veggie burgers—Beyond Burgers will be in the meat department if the store carries them.

Supermarkets are getting new foods in all the time, so if they don't have what you're looking for one week, you may want to try again in a week or two. If you're feeling up to it, you can make a recommendation to the manager that they try to get a certain product. Grocery stores are all about making money and keeping their customers happy, so if they see enough demand for something, they'll be open to trying it in their store.

When you're done shopping, keep all your receipts so you know much certain items cost and then you can compare prices to other grocery stores. If you save your receipts, you'll also be able to get an idea of how much a vegan diet will cost you long-term, and if it turns out to be too expensive, you'll know which areas to tackle to get those expenses down. Once you've loaded everything into your cabinets and refrigerator, you'll be stocked up and ready to start transitioning to your new diet.

What to Do With the Meat and Other Animal Products Already in Your Kitchen

What you do with the meat and other animal products that are already in your kitchen is up to you and depends largely on your transition plan.

One option is to give everything away to someone else who will eat it. If you're going vegan overnight, you won't want those items sitting around in your house. Their presence may be too tempting for you, or you may simply not want them anymore. If you know someone who isn't picky with their food, try giving all your meat and other animal foods to them. If you explain to them that you're going to try a vegan diet and don't want the food you've already purchased to go to waste, they'll probably be happy to take it off your hands. If you can't give it all to one person, ask a few people. Fortunately most people won't say no to free food—as long as it's something they like or if they're open to trying something new. If you can't find anyone willing to take your unwanted food items, look into donating everything to a local food pantry or soup kitchen.

Another option is to throw everything in the trash. This may not be your first choice, but it's certainly an option. Most people don't like to waste food, especially considering all the people in this world who are truly starving and suffering, but depending on where you are in your vegan journey, you may not want these products in your home. If you're unable to give the food away and you're adamant about not having it in your home, you can throw it away. If you don't have much meat or other animal products remaining in your home to begin with, it won't be a big deal. No one likes to waste food, but in this case, you have good reason. One chicken breast, a few eggs, and half a quart of milk is nothing compared to the resources wasted should you continue to eat these products regularly. If throwing a bit of food out is what helps you maintain your commitment to transitioning to a vegan diet, it's worth it. The animals are already dead. You're not doing them a disservice by "letting them go to waste." Corpses are generally buried, not thrown in the trash. You can bury your remaining meat and other animal products if you don't deem the dumpster to be respectful enough of a final resting place for the animals that made that food.

Lastly, you could continue to eat the animal products in your house until they're gone. The problem with this option is that it does little to break the bonds of "addiction" and to reprogram your brain with new habits. This tactic may work for some but not for others. You can try it to see how it works for you. If you feel compelled to continue buying more animal products, you'll know this may not be your best option. Sometimes in order to truly step away from something we need to put our foot down. Sometimes we need to declare a firm and unwavering "NO" to the things we don't want in order to pave a smoother path for the things we do want to welcome into our experience. A strong intent and conviction yields better results than when we're wishy-washy. For many people, setting a specific goal with a firm deadline is necessary for success.

If you don't want to waste the animal foods you have in your house and you feel confident you can slowly chip away at them until they're gone, without buying more, then continue to eat what you have until everything is gone. You can begin to settle into the right frame of mind to set you up for the greatest chance of success. When you're eating your last hotdogs, don't focus on how much you're going to miss them. Instead focus on how hotdogs are nothing more than a mash of the undesired parts of a cow or a pig, and the taste you enjoy is more from the spices and added condiments than anything else. When you're eating your last block of cheese, don't think about how you'll never be able to live without cheese for the rest of your life. Think about how that cheese was once squeezed out of an animal's body and that animal is most likely dead now. Think about how there are many different types of vegan hotdogs, sausages, and cheeses on the market and try to look forward to taste-testing all of them in the near future.

If you don't want to eat the rest of your animal products, you don't know anyone who is willing to take them, and you don't want them to go to waste, you may be able to feed them to a pet or leave them outside for other animals. Tuna, salmon, or other fish would be perfect for your cat. Beef or chicken can be left in the woods for coyotes or carrion birds. No matter what animal foods you have, if you leave them in the woods with the package removed, eventually some critter will find it and put it to good use.

If you're unable to rid your home of meat and other animal products because other members of your family won't be joining you on your transition, try to put all those items in a separate drawer or a separate cabinet from your vegan food so that it won't be on your mind, either tempting you or causing you to feel disgusted. If your family isn't willing to make the transition with you and you find it too tempting when they're eating animal foods in front of you, can try cooking separately and eating separately, at least for a while until you feel you're more in control. You may need to try a few different things until you find what works for you.

Transitioning

Do you have a set timeframe for your transition? Again this is where quitting meat and animal products is similar to quitting smoking. Many people have the best luck quitting cold turkey. They smoke their last cigarette and then they are done—no more, no matter what. Other people need to set a date in the near future to give themselves ample time to mentally prepare for that date. Some people need to slowly cut down on their consumption for a week or two before they feel they can transition completely.

Only you can figure out which kind of person you are, if you don't already know. If quitting overnight is too much pressure for you and you know you're setting yourself up for failure, then try giving yourself a week to transition.

No matter how much time you allot for the transition, do your best to mentally prepare yourself and to develop a positive mindset. If you're excited for the week and can't wait to get started trying new vegan foods and recipes, you're setting yourself up for success and your transition will be easier.

Cold ~~Turkey~~ Tofurky

What do you do when a turkey is left outside in the cold? You bring her inside and warm her up. You don't hesitate and you don't waste time watching her shiver. Quitting anything is like leaving your pet turkey out in the cold. You want to warm her up as quickly as possible, so you bring her inside immediately. Cold turkey is the way to go.

The name for this method should be changed from "cold turkey" to "cold Tofurky." Why? Because not bringing your cold pet turkey inside to warm up immediately isn't very nice. Who would leave her outside to suffer in the cold? Even the thought of leaving a poor turkey outside to shiver isn't pleasant. We can all pretend she was never left out in the cold to begin with and call it cold Tofurky instead.

When quitting cold Tofurky, you will definitely not want to have any meat or animal products in the house. Can you imagine your odds of success at quitting smoking if you had a pack of cigarettes and a lighter in your pocket at all times? At the first sign of a craving you'd pull one out and light up. If you're quitting cold Tofurky, make sure all things that might tempt you are absent. If your family is continuing to eat meat and animal products, work something out with them to at least keep it all away from you for a while. It's easier to quit smoking when there aren't other people in the room lighting up in front of you. Likewise it'll be easier going vegan when your family isn't eating bacon cheeseburgers in front of you at the dining room table while you're picking away at a salad.

When quitting cold Tofurky, realize that you may have strong cravings for the food you're used to eating. Realize that your mind may try to fight you and offer you 1,000 reasons why you need to eat meat, cheese, and eggs *right this minute!* Addictions tend to do the talking for us until we've had time away to let our own rational voices speak over them. Meat and other animal products may not have the same addictive properties as Nicotine and other drugs, but any strong daily habit can become an addiction after a long period of time. The absence of an addictive substance doesn't necessarily mean the habit will be easy to kick.

If you're unable to quit cold Tofurky, that's okay. You can take some time to transition into the lifestyle change as long as you're dedicated to it and your pet turkey isn't all alone outside shivering in the cold.

One Item

If the thought of transitioning to a vegan diet still seems daunting to you and you have doubts about your ability to transition within a single week, try starting with just one item. Pick one thing you eat daily or almost daily and substitute that one thing with a vegan version. For example, if you drink a glass of cow's milk with breakfast every morning, start by replacing that with plant milk instead. Try a few different plant milks until you find one you like. Once you begin to realize the substitute milk isn't bad, it may be time to move on to two items each day. You'll want to pick something that you consume often. A few suggestions are: cow's milk, coffee creamer, butter, yogurt, cream cheese, mayonnaise, or honey.

It must be something you use every day or nearly every day. Something simple and easily replaceable, so the absence of the animal version will have minimal impact on your everyday life. Swapping butter with vegan butter is a great example of a "one item" change. The difference in taste is negligible, if any. Once you see that your life will go on without cow butter and the quality of your life has not been negatively impacted by its absence, you'll have more confidence when the time comes to take the next step.

When one item swap proves not to be a big deal, consider adding a second item swap or even two more at once. With two or three items successfully swapped out with vegan versions, you're ready for the next step.

One Meal

With this method, you'll begin by having one fully vegan meal each day. Decide which meal will be best for you. Some people might prefer enjoying a vegan breakfast, especially if they're already inclined to eat cereal or oatmeal for breakfast, whereas diehard bacon and eggs folk might prefer swapping out a vegan lunch so they can still eat their favorite breakfast. If you want to swap out one meal each day but insist it must be a smaller meal, try swapping out a snack or dessert. It's only one small meal, but it will help put you in the daily habit of seeking out and preparing vegan food. If you choose dessert as your first meal to replace and you pick tasty, satisfying desserts, you'll be reinforcing the message to your brain that vegan desserts are no less delicious or satisfying than non-vegan desserts. If you're the type to enjoy a cup of ice cream every night for dessert, pick a tasty vegan ice cream you'll enjoy equally. This will send a message to your brain every evening that "This vegan ice cream is delicious!" and "Maybe vegan food isn't so bad!"

The key to this is that you swap out the same meal every day. This will effectively begin the process of replacing your old eating habits with new ones. Once you feel comfortable with one daily vegan meal, try switching another. Then you'll have a vegan breakfast and a vegan dessert every night, or a vegan snack and a vegan lunch every day. You don't have to eat the same exact meal every single day, but make sure it's around the same time each day so that you can continue to reinforce the new habit of enjoying vegan meals. The more fun and exciting you make these meals, the more you'll look forward to them each day, further reinforcing your new way of eating.

One Day

If you don't think you can consistently manage to eat one or two vegan meals every single day, try eating entirely vegan for one day each week. This will differ from the one meal approach in that instead of having a whole week filled with vegan breakfast and dessert, you have one fully vegan day and then it's over. Then you can eat whatever you want for 6 more days before you eat vegan food again. This method is less likely to reinforce new vegan meal habits, but it will give you an idea of what it's like to be vegan full time, every meal, even if only for one day.

The best way to increase your success with this method is by the time the second week rolls around, plan to eat entirely vegan for two days (in a row is best) this time instead of one. Then when you hit your third week, aim for three vegan days in a row. Or two vegans days in a row, then skip a day and go back to eating all vegan the next day. On your vegan days, you'll be less tempted to cheat because you know in another day or two you can eat whatever you want. If you're vegan for two or three full days in a particular week, you'll begin to get a sense of meal timing, how long it takes to cook certain dishes, and how much you must eat before feeling satiated. You'll begin to see how much eating vegan will cost each week, and you'll start to think like a full-time vegan. On your fourth week, try adding another day or two, and so on until you've completed the transition. If you're able to follow this method, you'll be fully switched and acclimated to a vegan diet in about four to six weeks.

One Week

One week is an ideal transition time. Since most people buy only enough groceries to last one week, with this transition timeframe, you'll be phasing out the animal products at the same speed in which you would have normally consumed them. One week gives you time to adjust while you finish up whatever you still have on hand and you phase in the new vegan food.

Taking a week to transition will also help you ease into preparing vegan meals on a daily basis. You'll have time to find new recipes, try new foods, experiment with different vegan cheeses, and shift into a new diet without the sudden immersion into veganism by quitting meat and dairy cold Tofurky.

One week is also the perfect length of time for meal prep. If you're concerned about how you'll handle all the cooking as you transition, you can easily do meal prep for the whole week by cooking in large batches. That will take some of the pressure off of you to figure out what to cook every day. If you can't meal prep for a full week, meal prep for five days. Then you'll only have to figure out what to make on the weekend, when you're likely to have more free time anyway.

By the end of the week, you'll probably have finished all the non-vegan food in your house and you'll be prepared to continue your vegan diet. However, by the end of the week if you feel you're not ready or you still have animal products on hand, you can extend the week by a day or two. You can lengthen your transition timeframe to two weeks if you need to. Lengthening your transition timeframe only because you're putting off going vegan won't help you in the long run, but if you have a good reason to take longer to transition, this may help ensure you're adequately prepared. If your house is stocked with meat and dairy products you don't want to go to waste, or if you're having trouble finding meals or recipes you think you'll enjoy, lengthening your transition timeframe can give you the extra time needed to solve these problems.

One Month

Taking an entire month to transition to a vegan diet will probably be too long for most people. By the end of the month, you'll have lost much of your motivation and your old habits will probably still be doing most of the talking. On the other hand, for people with serious food allergies, food sensitivities, or restricted diets, taking up to a month to transition may help them do it safely without causing any medical issues. They'll be able to experiment with new foods, weed out anything that doesn't agree with them, and slowly adjust to dietary changes. People with allergies to gluten, soy, nuts, legumes, or other foods may need to try a larger array of plant foods before they can pinpoint what causes them problems.

Another reason it may be a good idea to take up to a month to transition is for people who are suffering from severe "detox" symptoms. Detox symptoms are ways in which your body responds to changes in the food you're feeding it. People are creatures of habit and our bodies can become accustomed to certain foods. When those foods are taken away and replaced, the body notices the absence of what it has become used to and mild to severe symptoms may result. These symptoms are not necessarily due to toxins leaving the body. They may be nothing more than signs you body is adjusting. Many people experience a variety of detox symptoms, and others don't experience any noticeable symptoms whatsoever. Some possible symptoms may include: headache, fatigue, excess gas, gastrointestinal disruption, which may include excess trips to the bathroom (can be caused by dietary changes and/or increased fiber consumption), food cravings, and mood swings. True detox symptoms rarely last more than 3-5 days. If detox symptoms last more than a week during your transition to a vegan diet, the symptoms may be from something else entirely, such as insufficient calorie, protein, or fat intake. We'll cover those issues more closely later in this book.

How Long Should Your Vegan Challenge Last?

For the rest of your life. That's it...end of the book.

What? Too daunting? Okay, we can discuss other options. The length of time you set for your vegan challenge should not be too short. It needs to be long enough for you to learn new eating habits and get comfortable with them. A week or two is far too short to develop new habits, and you'll barely scratch the surface of trying all the delicious plants foods and phenomenal recipes floating around out there. If you go vegan for a week or two and don't really know how to structure your meals, you may eat too few calories and/or protein and feel depressed, hungry, and tired. After the end of the week or two, you'll feel like the challenge failed and perhaps believe a vegan diet isn't for you. It takes time to settle into a new diet and two weeks is not long enough. Three weeks is the bare minimum length of time you should allot to testing out a vegan diet. Even then, three weeks is relatively short.

Three Weeks (Challenge 22+)

The reason three weeks is the bare minimum is because a lifetime of eating habits cannot be entirely reconstructed in a week or two.

The website Challenge22.com is a wonderful resource for anyone interested in committing to a vegan diet for a period of 22 days or more. Launched in March 2014, the challenge was created by Animals Now, an Israeli non-profit organization established in 1994. The main page of the website offers a brief description of how the challenge works. First, anyone interested in taking the challenge must sign up by filling out a very short form. Then they'll receive an invitation to join a Facebook group of mentors and other

Challenge 22+ participants. Each day of the challenge, participants receive tips, recipes, videos, and simple challenges, such as learning to make a vegan sandwich, or going out to eat at a vegan restaurant. The Facebook group has mentors and certified clinical dieticians who are available to help "around the clock." The Challenge 22 website boasts that at the present time, 204,550 people have participated in the challenge.

For anyone interested in transitioning to a vegan diet who thinks they'll need help from a mentor and other people who have made or are currently making the transition, Challenge22.com is an invaluable resource. The extra support may be what some people need to successfully make the switch. The minimum length of the challenge is 22 days, but participants may wish to continue the challenge indefinitely.

One Month

Thirty day challenges have become popular in recent times. A search of books on Amazon will turn up a large number of different titles dedicated to 30 day challenges. Marc Reklau wrote the #1 Amazon bestseller '30 Days – Change Your Habits, Change Your Life'. Shaunti Feldhahn wrote 'The Kindness Challenge: Thirty Days to Improve Any Relationship'. There's even a book called the '30-Day Vegan

Challenge', by Colleen Patrick-Goudreau. Popular blogger Steve Pavlina has participated in a number of 30 day challenges that he's documented in great detail on his blog StevePavlina.com. From 30 days of polyphasic sleep (sleeping 20 minutes every 3 hours, for example) to 30 days at Disneyland, Steve Pavlina has taken on some of the most interesting 30 day challenges you'll find anywhere.

One of the most famous 30 day challenges ever documented was Morgan Spurlock's challenge of eating nothing but McDonald's food for an entire month, as documented by the popular 2004 film Super Size Me.

By comparison, eating vegan for 30 days is easier, healthier, and cheaper than eating fast food for a month. If at any point during your challenge you find yourself feeling frustrated or deprived, think about how much worse it would be if you could only order the same food off the same menu for an entire month. Fortunately when it comes to a vegan diet, the possibilities are practically limitless. There are tens of thousands of edible plant species in the world, yet most of us eat only a tiny fraction of them. Going vegan for a month is your chance to branch out and try new foods and new recipes. Going vegan isn't about depriving yourself. Spending a full 30 days (or more) devoted to a plant-based diet will begin to open doors for you in terms of all the delicious plant foods you're missing by regularly filling your belly with meat, cheese, and eggs.

One month vegan is enough time for you to rewire your brain with new eating habits, and it's also enough time for you to truly begin learning the joys of begin vegan. If you join a few vegan groups, try some new foods, and take time to learn about animal agriculture, you'll have a chance to fully immerse yourself in a vegan lifestyle and view the world through a lens of compassion, understanding, and concern for animals and the environment.

Two Months

Devoting an entire month to following a vegan diet is wonderful, but for some it's not long enough to truly delve into the lifestyle. There's a limit to the number of vegan restaurants you can visit, new recipes you can cook, and vegan friends you can make in a month. It's hardly enough time to try all the vegan cheeses and meats on the market, hardly enough time to make new friends and learn about their experiences on their own vegan journeys. Going vegan for 30 days is like trying to learn a new language in a month—you can make significant progress but you'll never be completely fluent in such a short timeframe. Two months may only be double the time, but most of your first month being devoted to simply figuring out how to make a vegan diet work for you.

This second month will be the period when you can relax a bit, knowing you've pretty much got it figured out. You won't need to stress when trying to decide what to cook next and what to buy at the grocery store. By now you've had a chance to make new friends, determine your likes and dislikes when it comes to vegan food, and learn about animal agriculture.

Consider these two months a deep dive into a vegan lifestyle. By the end of this challenge, it'll no longer be a mystery to you where to get your protein, how to eat vegan without spending a fortune, or why anyone would choose to stick with the lifestyle long-term. Your cravings for animal foods will likely have disappeared and you'll be feeling good about your new eating habits. You'll probably have learned useful cooking skills you can take with you for the rest of your life and utilize with any type of diet, anywhere you live. You'll have new friends who are ready and eager to cheer you on and help you with tips and suggestions should you continue living vegan long-term.

Three Months

By the end of three months of following a vegan diet, it will probably be easier for you to continue the lifestyle than it would be for you to go back to your old ways. At this point, as long as you haven't been unnecessarily depriving yourself or restricting your diet, you'll probably be wondering why it took you so long to go vegan to begin with. At three months, you'll have a good feel for living a vegan lifestyle and you'll be able to offer useful suggestions to others who are beginning to try veganism for the first time.

If you went vegan for health reasons, you may have begun to focus on other aspects of veganism as well, such as the impact animal agriculture has on the environment or the horrific treatment of animals during the process. Many people who go vegan for health reasons claim that they *later* began to feel concern and compassion for the animals.

Many people who stay vegan for this long will go on to stay vegan for a year or more. An object in motion tends to remain in motion.

Six Months to One Year

If you've stuck with a vegan diet for six months to a year, you're essentially a veteran at this point. You know what to eat, when to eat, and how much to eat. You no longer have any trouble keeping yourself feeling satiated (if you ever did), you've tried lots of new foods and new recipes, you've veganized your old favorite foods, you've made a few vegan friends, and you've probably delved into the ethical side of veganism, assuming that wasn't one of your prime motivators initially.

On the other side of the coin, if you went vegan for ethical reasons and paid little attention to whether the food you were consuming was healthy, by this point you've probably grown tired of all the junk food and you're making more of a conscious effort to eat better. If not, now's the time!

Staying vegan for the long run is a dual effort: going vegan for the sole purpose of improving your own personal health may prove to be a weak long-term motivator. Also, going vegan for the animals only with no concern for your own personal health can equally be a recipe for failure. If your health begins to deteriorate because of a junk food vegan diet, the animals may not be a strong enough motivator to stay the course, either. Many ex-vegans cite poor health as the reason they gave up the lifestyle. They believe the solution lies in the vitamins and minerals they're missing from meat and dairy, when in many cases their failing health is due to inadequate nutrition in their vegan diet. If you've been consuming little more than processed, frozen vegan meals, processed vegan meats and cheeses, non-dairy ice cream, crackers, and French fries for a year, your health may begin to fail. If and when this happens, many vegans will assume it's because there's a serious lack of nutrients in their diet due to the absence of meat and animal products. In fact, the lack of nutrients is most likely due to a lack of fruits, vegetables, legumes, and whole grains.

No matter what type of diet you're following (vegetarian, vegan, keto, paleo) if you're not eating a broad spectrum of different foods in a well-balanced diet, you're bound to start suffering from health problems eventually. No diet is 100% perfect. This is part of the reason why the vitamin and supplement industry is a $37 billion[6] a year business in the United States, according to the National Institutes of Health. That $37 billion per year isn't coming from pale, sick, weak vegans. It's coming from the majority of Americans following an unbalanced omnivorous diet.

NutritionFacts.org cites a 2010 report from the National Cancer Institute that found 75% of Americans don't eat a single piece of fruit in a given day, 90% don't reach the minimum recommended daily intake of vegetables, 96% don't reach the minimum intake for greens, and 99% of Americans don't reach the recommended minimum daily intake of whole grains. No wonder Americans are spending $37 billion per year on vitamins and supplements!

Whether you're vegan or not has little bearing on whether you're consuming a well-balanced diet. Many vegans who give up the diet and lifestyle do so because somewhere along the line their health began to deteriorate and they want to reclaim it. They assume the problem is that they're not eating meat, dairy, and eggs, but the problem could very well be that even as a vegan, they're not eating enough fruit, vegetables, and whole grains. It could also be that they're not getting enough protein. A person who followed a poor, unhealthy diet as an omnivore isn't necessarily going to follow a healthy, well-balanced diet as a vegan. If unhealthy vegans turn to an omnivorous diet to solve their health issues, and unhealthy omnivores turn to vitamins and supplements to solve their health issues (with limited success), where's the solution? The solution is to follow a diet most natural to human beings—a well-balanced diet rich in unprocessed plant foods such as fruits, vegetables, beans and legumes, whole grains, nuts and seeds.

Meal Structure

As mentioned earlier, the typical western diet is often seen as a large slab of meat, a generous portion of potatoes, pasta, or rice, and a meager serving of vegetables. We'll also have to throw cheese in there somewhere—on the potatoes perhaps? Why not also melt some butter on the vegetables, too, to make them more palatable? This is probably one of the healthier versions of the western diet you'll find. It's certainly better than fried chicken, French fries, and donuts.

This is not *the definitive* meal structure that must be mimicked with plant foods when going vegan. There's no ideal way to structure any diet, vegan included. Unless you're following a specific diet for specific goals, you do not need to follow a macronutrient breakdown of 60% carbohydrates, 20% protein, 20% fats, or any similar breakdown. Most people probably won't need to track any of these for any reason.

Your meals do not need to be structured in a certain way in order to be healthy. If you want to eat an entire plate of pasta for dinner and nothing else, do that. If you want to eat an entire watermelon for dinner, do that. If you want to eat rice and beans for breakfast and dark chocolate cinnamon raisin oatmeal for dinner, go ahead and do that. There's no ideal way to structure your meals unless you have very specific goals. All that matters is that you're eating a wide variety of healthy plant foods—fruits, vegetables, beans and legumes, whole grains, nuts and seeds. If you want to eat a mixture of all of those in one meal, that's fine. If you want to eat an entire meal consisting of only one of those items (two tubs of hummus for dinner, for example), that's fine too. As long as you're eating a well-balanced diet over the course of the day, each individual meal is far less important.

There's no unwritten (or written) law of veganism that mandates meals must be structured in a certain way. Your body will make the best use out of everything you put into it over the course of the day. Cheat meals are fine in moderation, or even frequently if you have no qualms about gaining a little weight. If you want to eat nothing but chocolate chip cookies for dinner one night of the week, go ahead and do it. As long as they've vegan chocolate chip cookies. You do not need to eat healthy 100% of the time.

If you believe each meal *must* consist of a protein, a carbohydrate, and a vegetable, you're limiting yourself. If you eat an entire pound of cooked cauliflower, followed by a can of drained, rinsed black beans, you're consuming a very healthy meal, regardless of the unorthodox structuring of the meal. A meal of nothing but brown rice and beans is quite healthy, despite the lack of vegetables and healthy fats. The vegetables and healthy fats can be in your next meal. For the most part, you can eat what you want, when you want, as long as you're eating a wide variety of predominantly healthy, nutritious plant foods over the course of the day, week, and month.

Calorie Consumption

Consuming insufficient calories is one of the biggest problems among new vegans. This is due, in part, to the common misconception that vegans only eat vegetables and salad. Meat and most animal products are a dense source of calories. When those calories are taken away, some new and inexperienced vegans may not fully understand how to replace those missing calories. Looking back once again to our plate that consists of a slab of meat, a pile of potatoes, and a few bites of vegetables, the first tendency of a new vegan may be to simply nix the meat and eat the rest of the plate. They'll be hungry afterward because they're not replacing that source of dense calories with a similar vegan source of dense calories. This is the worst thing a new vegan can do.

A marginally better option would be to increase the pile of potatoes to make up for the missing slab of meat. Potatoes may be relatively dense in calories, but not in comparison to the meat. One 4 ounce portion of steak has about 300 calories, but 4 ounces of potatoes will only deliver about 90 calories. You'd have to eat nearly a pound of potatoes to match the calories in one 4 ounce portion of steak. You're going to be stuffed before you finish the potatoes and you'll still be at a calorie deficit, meaning you're going to be hungry again soon. If you continue this pattern, you'll lose weight and you'll be hungry constantly. A vegan diet will prove to be unsustainable for you and you'll probably quit and go back to eating meat, dairy, and eggs. Who could blame you?

On the other hand, if you were to replace that 4 ounce steak with 4 ounces of cooked lentils, you'll be getting 400 calories. A cup of cooked split peas will offer around 300 calories, and so will a cup of cooked black beans. A better idea would be to keep the pile of potatoes, increase the serving of vegetables by several times, and then toss in the lentils or beans.

The meal doesn't *need* to be structured that way as long as you're getting enough calories and fiber to fill you up and keep you satiated until your next meal. You can throw some brown rice, quinoa, and vegetables into a pot and cook it all together. Afterward, you can add an avocado and some hot sauce. As long as you're consuming enough calories along with enough fibrous bulk to keep you full, you should be fine.

For help in determining if you're consuming enough calories, try taking a Total Daily Energy Expenditure (TDEE) test. This will tell you how many calories you need to maintain your current bodyweight at your current activity levels. From there, you'll want to count your calories for a week or so to make sure you're at least hitting that number, provided your goal is to maintain bodyweight.

Protein Consumption

Only you can determine your protein needs. Some vegans will tell you all you need is 46 grams per day for the average woman and 56 grams per day for the average man. Other vegans will tell you protein isn't important and you don't need to monitor your intake. The truth is how much protein you need to consume each day depends on your specific needs.

If you don't get much exercise and you're fine with that, 50-60 grams of protein per day might be sufficient for you. However, if you're highly active with any combination of regular sports, hiking, weightlifting, calisthenics, intense cardiovascular exercise, or even a physically demanding job, you're going to need more protein. The recommended protein requirements for highly active individuals are all over the board, depending on which source you're following.

Old-school bodybuilders swear you must consume at least one gram of protein per pound of bodyweight per day. That would be a minimum of 200 grams of protein per day for a 200 pound man trying to gain muscle mass. Other sources will claim that's too high, and that 100 to 150 grams per day would be sufficient for that 200 pound man.

The best thing you can do to determine how much protein you need each day is to start by taking a TDEE test, which will tell you how many calories you must consume to maintain bodyweight. Depending on the specific TDEE test, it may also offer you suggestion for the amount of protein to consume. To more accurately determine the amount of protein you need, first make sure you're hitting your calorie recommendation.

Chances are good that if you're following a mostly whole foods plant-based diet and you're consuming enough calories, you're also getting enough protein. However, if your activity level is higher than average, it won't hurt to consume extra protein. You can do this by replacing lower protein foods (such as rice) with higher protein foods (such as quinoa or lentils), or by supplementing protein in the form of hemp protein powder, rice powder, or a mixed powder such as Vega or Sunwarrior.

Another way to determine whether you're getting enough protein is to go by how you feel. If you've had a heavy weight workout and/or an intense cardio session, your body will be screaming for protein. If you're still hungry after eating a large, filling meal, you're probably not getting enough protein to fill your needs. Signs of inadequate protein consumption can be: fatigue, depression, fluid retention, hair loss, loss of strength or muscle mass and constant hunger. Constant hunger is one of the most reliable signs, and it's the one most commonly associated with food intake. Hair loss, depression, or fatigue can easily be mistaken as symptoms of vitamin deficiency or some other ailment, but if you're constantly hungry no matter how much you eat, chances are good that you're not consuming enough protein. New vegans may mistakenly believe the lack of animal products is the culprit when all they need to do is consume more vegan protein.

If you've ever heard that you must combine proteins (rice and beans, peanut butter and whole wheat, corn and quinoa) to get a full amino acid profile into each meal, forget that. The incomplete protein theory is a myth. The protein combining myth was popularized by the 1971 book, *Diet for a Small Planet*, by Frances Moore Lappé. The human body stores amino acids, so consuming a complete amino acid profile with each meal is unnecessary. The author has corrected this misinformation in more recent editions of the book. Eating a wide variety of plant foods during the course of the day will ensure you're receiving all the amino acids your body needs.

Another myth concerning protein is that plant proteins aren't as "bioavailable" as animal-based proteins, and this, in part, is why vegans can't build muscle as effectively as omnivores or vegetarians. According to Vicki Shanta Retelny, RDN[7], a nutritionist from Chicago, IL, the amino acids in plants are just as bioavailable as the amino acids in animal proteins. One thing to note is that research has shown that the proteins from whole plant foods may be *slightly* less digestible than animal-based proteins due to the high fiber content inhibiting absorption. This is only to a small degree, an estimated 10 to 20% at most. Plant proteins may be slightly less digestible than animal proteins, but the notion that plant proteins have inferior bioavailability is a myth.

If you still believe vegans can't build as much muscle as meat eaters, check out VeganBodybuilding.com. Founded in 2002 by Robert Cheeke, the website is one of the best resources available for anyone interested in gaining muscle on a vegan diet. Robert Cheeke adopted a vegan lifestyle in 1995 and became interested in weightlifting in 1999. He became a competitive bodybuilder in 2000, and after 20 years of being a vegan bodybuilder, he shows no signs of slowing down. A Google image search of Cheeke shows that after decades of following a vegan diet, he doesn't seem to be suffering from a lack of protein or proper nutrition. For anyone interested in vegan bodybuilding, check out all the information available on his website.

There are other popular vegan bodybuilders and athletes, such as: Torre Washington, Derek Tresize, Vanessa Espinoza, Dani Taylor, Nimai Delgado, Brian Turner, and Patrik Baboumian. Patrik Baboumian is a multiple world record holding strength athlete who has been vegan since 2011. These athletes have clearly demonstrated that they have no trouble getting enough protein. If they can consume adequate protein on a vegan diet, anyone can.

Fat Consumption

There are many sources of healthy fats on a vegan diet and as long as you're eating a wide variety of foods, you're not likely to suffer from problems associated with consuming insufficient fat. Nuts, nut butters, seeds, avocadoes, olive oil and other vegetable oils, mayonnaise, and coconuts are all high in healthy fats. Oats, quinoa, soy, beans, and legumes also have a fair amount of fat. People most susceptible to symptoms of consuming insufficient fat are those following a raw vegan diet or an otherwise fat-restricted diet. Symptoms of consuming insufficient fat may include: dry skin, cracking/peeling skin, dandruff, dry eyes, dry mouth or throat, brittle fingernails, stiff or painful joints, and strong cravings for fatty foods. If you're following a low-fat diet and you start to suffer from these symptoms, begin incorporating healthy fats back into your diet. Symptoms should begin to improve within a few days if your diet was to blame.

Vitamins to Watch

One of the main concerns new vegans and transitioning vegans have with following a plant-based diet is the supposed lack of certain nutrients and the fear they'll develop a deficiency which will lead to health problems. Often new vegans will state that they've been experiencing symptoms such as fatigue, headaches, dizziness, weakness, or depression, after being vegan for a certain length of time (generally a couple weeks to a couple months) and ask if they may be suffering from a vitamin deficiency.

It should be noted that some vegans do not supplement whatsoever and even after years of following a plant-based diet, they still show no signs of deficiency when having their blood tested. This is not the case with all vegans, nor is it clear if this is *possible* for all vegans. As individuals and individual diets vary greatly, there's no way to determine ahead of time who will develop deficiencies and who will not. This is why it's best to supplement certain vitamins and minerals, in addition to making every effort to consume foods rich in these particular nutrients. Supplementing is cheap and easy— there's no reason not to.

B-12

The vitamin people most commonly associate with their symptoms is B-12. According to the National Health Service of the United Kingdom, B-12 stores in the human body can last 2 to 4 years without being replenished[8]. This means that new vegans who are suffering from any of the above symptoms are not likely to be suffering from a deficiency of vitamin B-12.

Vitamin B-12 is very important and long-term deficiency can have serious health consequences. Though it may take 2 to 4 for your body's B-12 stores to become depleted, there's no reason to wait that long without doing anything about it. Taking B-12 supplements absolutely cannot hurt, and they're quite inexpensive, so there's no reason *not* to take them. Even people who eat meat can be low in vitamin B-12 and eventually develop a deficiency. It's better to be safe than sorry in this case, so if you're following a vegan diet, you might as well take a B-12 supplement. One dose per week should be enough, especially if you're eating fortified foods, but it won't hurt to take more. Foods often fortified with B-12 include nutritional yeast, some soy products, and certain cereals and plant milks. Nutritional yeast is usually B-12 fortified, and since it's a common vegan cheese alternative, many vegans get enough of the vitamin from a combination of nutritional yeast and other fortified foods as listed above. It's difficult to take *too much* B-12 as the human body excretes whatever it doesn't use through urine, so feel free to take a supplement in addition to consuming fortified foods. If you have reason to think your levels are low, having your blood tested might be a good idea.

Iron

Iron deficiency can also cause similar symptoms, and as with vitamin B-12, iron deficiency also takes a long time to develop. It's very unlikely that a person who has been vegan for only a few weeks or a few months is suffering from iron deficiency due to their change in diet. In any case, to alleviate some worry, be sure to consume plenty of foods that are high in iron.

- Black beans
- Blackstrap molasses
- Brown rice
- Cashews
- Chard
- Chickpeas
- Kale
- Lentils
- Oats
- Quinoa
- Soy
- Spinach
- Sunflower seeds

The foods on this list are all high in iron. Making these and other high iron foods a part of your daily diet will help to ensure you're consuming enough. There are vegan iron supplements available that will help to boost your levels if you suspect you're low. Iron supplements can take a couple weeks to boost the levels in your blood. If you have reason to suspect your iron levels are low, it might be best to have your blood tested so you can know for sure.

Vitamin D

Few foods contain vitamin D naturally. Mushrooms are the number one plant food for vitamin D. Leaving mushrooms out in the sunlight for even a short period of time will boost their vitamin D content[9]. Aside from mushrooms, most other foods containing vitamin D will have been fortified. Tofu, soy milk, and orange juice are foods that are often fortified with the vitamin.

The human body makes vitamin D from exposure to sunlight. Research suggests that as little as 15 to 30 minutes of sun exposure twice per week[10] is sufficient for the body to make enough vitamin D.

If you decide to supplement vitamin D, try to find one that is certified vegan. Vitamin D_2 is derived from plant sources and vitamin D_3 can be derived from either plant or animal sources. So if you're concerned about from where your vitamin D is sourced, look for a supplement that is certified vegan.

Omega-3 Fatty Acids

Plant foods high in omega-3 fatty acids include flax seeds, chia seeds, hemp seeds, walnuts, soybeans, seaweed, kale, basil, Brussels sprouts, cauliflower, and canola oil.

Research suggests that vegans and vegetarians have significantly lower blood concentrations of long-chain omega-3 fatty acids (EPA and DHA)[11] despite that the body converts essential omega-3 fatty acids (ALA) into EPA and DHA. Many vegans choose to supplement these long-chain omega-3 fatty acids. Vegan EPA and DHA supplements are derived from algae and there are several vegan EPA and DHA products available on the market for anyone wishing to supplement.

Calcium

The dairy industry would like you to believe that the best (if not the *only*) source of calcium is cow's milk, cheese, yogurt, and other dairy products. More recent research suggests that the calcium in dairy products is not well assimilated by the human body and that the consumption of animal proteins may increase the acidity of blood, which causes the body to pull calcium from bones to neutralize the acid. More conclusive research is needed to either prove or disprove these theories, however, it is quite possible that cow's milk and other dairy products not only fail to strengthen teeth and bones, as the dairy industry would have you believe, but that these products actually contribute to osteoporosis. For more information on how dairy consumption affects bone health, read The China Study.

Plant foods that are high in calcium include soy, beans, lentils, peas, seeds, seaweed, kale, spinach, broccoli, Brussels sprouts, blackstrap molasses, and fortified foods such as plant milks, cereal, and bread. Blackstrap molasses is a sweetener made from sugar cane and one tablespoon provides up to 20% of the recommended daily intake of both calcium and iron. Blackstrap molasses are great for adding to oatmeal, not only for extra sweetness but also for the added nutritional value.

Iodine

Studies suggest that vegans have lower iodine levels than meat eaters and vegetarians[12]. Seaweed and kelp absorb iodine from seawater and are excellent sources for vegans. Iodized salt is packed with iodine but consuming high levels of sodium daily can be harmful to your health. Iodized salt is best consumed in moderation.

Other plant foods high in iodine are cranberries, potatoes, corn, prunes, and strawberries. If you're not consuming enough iodine from these plant foods, seaweed, and iodized salt, you may want to consider taking an iodine supplement.

Zinc

Zinc is an essential nutrient required by the human body. It's also one of the most abundant metals in the body, second only to iron. Zinc deficiency can lead to nasty symptoms such as impotence, delayed wound healing, diarrhea, mental fatigue, and hair loss.

The following foods are high in zinc:

- Beans
- Chia seeds
- Flax seeds
- Fortified cereals
- Hemp seeds
- Lentils
- Mushrooms
- Oats
- Peas
- Pumpkin seeds
- Quinoa
- Spinach
- Tofu

Vegans who are unable to reach the recommended daily intake of zinc should consider taking a daily supplement.

Takeout/Dining Out

During your transition to a vegan diet, you're bound to get tired of cooking and need a break eventually. Or, if your significant other does most of the cooking, he or she is bound to get tired of cooking at some point. Even vegans who *love* to cook need a break now and then. If you and/or your partner despise cooking and you're prone to "preparing" packaged, processed food rather than cooking your own food, you're eventually going to want a break from that as well. This is where dining out and takeout food comes into play.

Takeout

In the United States, the most common takeout foods are fast food, Chinese food, and pizza. Many of the traditional fast food restaurants in the U.S. have limited vegan and vegetarian options. You may be limited to little more than French fries at most of the burger joints in the U.S., and that's assuming the French fries at your favorite burger joint aren't cooked in beef tallow. Are the fries cooked in the same oil that's also used to fry meat products? This is something you'll definitely want to research online before ordering fast food.

Burger King offers a veggie burger, but it's not vegan. They will soon be offering the "Impossible Whopper" at all Burger King locations in the United States for a test run. Even then, many vegans refuse to eat Impossible Foods because the company has admitted to testing on animals in the past.

Taco Bell and other taco joints in the western United States have a fair amount of vegan options provided you specify without meat or cheese. A bean burrito with vegetables is vegan as long as no cheese, sour cream, or other dairy products are added. Chipotle Mexican Grill has many vegan options (which are listed on their website) and the company doesn't use eggs, fish, or shellfish in their food.

Subway isn't a bad choice for a quick bite. Vegan bread options at Subway are the Italian, Hearty Italian, Wrap, and Sourdough. The Veggie Delite is vegan as long as you order it without cheese, and you can load it up with as many veggies as you like, including the avocado or guacamole (which cost extra). Vegan sauces at Subway are the yellow mustard, brown mustard, oil and vinegar, fat-free Italian dressing, sweet onion sauce, buffalo sauce, and the Subway vinaigrette. You can also add a few of your own toppings to your sub afterward to make it more interesting and delicious, such as vegan cheese, vegan mayonnaise, cooked tempeh, or sliced vegan sausage. If cross-contamination is a concern for you, feel free to ask them to use a fresh pair of gloves when making your sandwich.

Chinese food and most Asian restaurants are excellent for vegan options, especially if you're not a stickler about cross-contamination. Just remember to ask if they use fish sauce in your dish, and if so, you can ask them to omit the sauce, or you can order something else. Nearly every Asian restaurant offers tofu as an alternative to meat in many of their dishes. Many Asian restaurants even have a separate section on their menu devoted to "vegetarian" food, which are often vegan due to the tendency of Asian restaurants not to use dairy or eggs in many of their dishes.

One of the reasons many people never consider switching to veganism is because of all the foods they mistakenly believe they'd have to "give up" when making the switch. There's no doubt that one of the top foods on the list of what they'd never be able to give up is pizza. Great news! There's no need to give up pizza! More independently owned and operated pizza places are offering vegan meats and cheeses than ever before. However, if your favorite pizza joint is lacking for vegan options, you can try bringing your own and ask them to add it to your pie. Some pizza places may not appreciate customers bringing in their own toppings, but other places don't mind as long as you're a paying customer. They're more likely to accommodate you if you're a frequent customer, but with the growth of veganism in recent years, many pizza places are recognizing the potential and hopping on the bandwagon. What difference does it make to them to toss on a few extra items a customer has brought? They may want to charge you a little more, so be prepared for that possibility.

If you can't find a pizza place that offers vegan options and no one is willing to toss vegan meat and cheese you supplied onto a pie for you, don't worry, you can still order a vegan pie from almost any pizza place. Almost all pizza dough consists of only flour, yeast, salt, olive oil, water, and possibly sugar. If you want to be absolutely certain their pizza dough is vegan, you can ask, but otherwise, the chances are very good that it will be. A simple red pie, without cheese, and loaded up with whichever vegetables you want is a perfectly good vegan pizza. One thing to watch out for is any vegetable topping (such as eggplant) that has been breaded and pan fried. You may want to ask them if they use any non-vegan ingredients in their breading or in the frying process. Otherwise, you can nix the breaded and fried veggie options and stick to plain vegetables.

Different pizza places will have different options when it comes to vegetables as toppings. Many pizza places that specialize in certain pies that are heavily laden with meat may have a limited selection of vegetable toppings. One of the most famous and most popular pizza joints in this area offers only five or six vegetables as toppings—and that's if you count garlic and onions as vegetables. Other places offer specialty veggie pies to keep the vegans and vegetarians happy. Don't forget to tell them you want "no cheese at all" otherwise they may hold the mozzarella but sprinkle parmesan on top of your pie. Nothing ruins a nice cheeseless vegan pizza pie like seeing an unasked for and unnecessary sprinkling of parmesan cheese.

Dining Out

If you're transitioning to a vegan diet, you're bound to want to get out and eat a hearty meal at a nice restaurant eventually, so it will help to have a few restaurants in mind. Search Google or HappyCow.net for vegan restaurants in your area, and regular restaurants that offer vegan options. Consider yourself lucky if you have at least one vegan restaurant within 30 minutes from you as many people don't have even that.

If you had a favorite restaurant before you began your transition, check out their menu and their website to find out what sort of vegan options they offer. If you see nothing on the menu or on the website, try to get creative. Many restaurants will be happy to accommodate you if you tell them what you cannot eat, or if you ask them what they can whip together for you that is vegan. Restaurants that don't have vegan options on the menu are likely to have been asked by other customers before you what they have that's vegan. They may already have a few ideas of what they can cook to accommodate you even if their menu doesn't look promising.

Restaurants are adapting to the growing vegan demand and many places that did not previously offer vegan options are changing with the times and adding options and sometimes even dedicated vegan menus. If your favorite restaurant has nothing of the sort, it's possible they may already be working on changing that, and one or two more people asking for vegan options may prompt them to make the switch. Restaurants know they have to change with the times or else they risk being left behind.

Get-Togethers

What should you do if you're invited to a party, holiday dinner, or a meal out with friends during your transition? If you find transitioning to a vegan diet to be challenging and you're worried that you may be tempted to "cheat" you have a few options to help keep you on track.

If you're going out to eat at a restaurant, see if you can compromise by going to a place that has an abundance of vegan options. If you're looking at the menu of a restaurant while out to eat with friends and you see no vegan options, you don't want to have to be stuck between the tough choice of either eating nothing or ordering a non-vegan meal. If you plan to order a non-vegan meal "just this once" not only will you have to start all over again the next day, but you'll also feel guilty for eating non-vegan food. Additionally, depending on how far along you are in your transition, it's quite possible that eating non-vegan food at this point may make you feel sick to your stomach. On the other hand, if you're at a restaurant that offers several vegan dishes, you should be able to find something you can eat and not have to be tempted to order food that isn't vegan. Another option would be to eat before the meal and go only for the company and the conversation.

If you're going to a holiday meal or a party at someone's home where you know they'll be few (if any) vegan options, why not bring your own food? Or better yet, bring lots of food to share with everyone else. This is an excellent way to turn people on to vegan food, especially if what you bring tastes great and approximates a non-vegan dish that people love, like pizza, lasagna, or chili to name a few examples. Many non-vegans still have the mistaken belief that vegan food is bland, boring, and consists of nothing but vegetables and salad. If you bring a dish like "meaty" lasagna, loaded pizza, or creamy macaroni and cheese, you'll be showing them that not only is vegan food delicious, but you're not missing out on anything and you didn't have to give up your favorite foods when you went vegan.

Another less popular option that some vegans prefer is to not go to these get-togethers at all. Some vegans don't want to be around meat consumption so they opt out of these sorts of events, preferring vegan parties with other like-minded people. If you're attending an all-vegan party or holiday meal, you'll be able to eat anything there. If everyone brings a vegan dish, you'll have no trouble filling up on lots of different foods. If there are certain vegan foods you don't like, you'll be able to avoid those items while still having lots of other stuff to choose from.

Eating With Non-Vegan Friends and Family

Vegans are somewhat divided when it comes to eating with non-vegan friends and family. Many vegans are neutral when it comes to meat consumption and see nothing wrong with another person's choice to eat meat. They may have no qualms about dining with people while they eat meat and other animal products. Some vegans are less neutral when it comes to animal consumption, but still enjoy eating with non-vegan friends and family because it gives them the opportunity to talk about veganism, share food, and perhaps interest others in checking out a vegan diet.

On the other hand, many vegans are disgusted by the smell of meat and other animal products and choose not to be around when these things are being consumed. When invited to a non-vegan party or meal, they will politely decline, even if it's a holiday meal with beloved family. They may see meat eating as something that should be shunned instead of normalized and accepted. They see animals as dear friends and thus don't want to be around while they're being eaten.

This difference of opinion is responsible for a bit of a division among vegans, but no one is "right" and no one is "wrong." The truth is that everyone is different and opinions will differ no matter what. If you're fine with others eating meat even though you are vegan, that's who you are, or, at least how you feel about the issue at this stage of your vegan journey. You may not want to "push your views" on others and take no issue with what they eat or how they live their lives. You are not wrong.

Maybe you're not okay with others eating meat but you still want to eat with them in hopes you can influence them with your ideas and your delicious vegan food. That's fine, too.

If you're new to veganism and you're transitioning, you probably won't mind so much that others continue to eat meat and animal products. Going vegan and being vegan is very much a journey, however, and a person's views tend to evolve and change over time. If you eventually find yourself detesting meat and refusing to be around while it's being consumed, you are not wrong, either. Nor are you alone. Many vegans feel this way. A common belief in this school of thought is that by politely refusing to eat with non-vegans, vegans are demonstrating how important this issue is to them. They want to see change when it comes to the consumption of animals and they don't want to demonstrate support or tolerance of the very thing they wish to change. These vegans see little difference between hurting animals for food versus hurting animals for fun—and as they would not sit and chat with someone who is abusing a dog, they refuse to sit and chat with someone who is consuming a pig or a cow.

No one here is wrong. As everyone is different, their beliefs will differ. Do whatever feels right to you during the various stages of your journey.

Beyond the Diet

This book is mainly about transitioning to a vegan diet, but there's so much more to being vegan than what we eat. If you wish to pursue veganism further than your diet alone, this part of the book will help explain the hows and the whys of animal exploitation beyond what we eat.

There seems to be this prevailing notion that as long as we "use all of an animal" it's okay to kill them. As if letting a dead animal's corpse go to waste (by being buried in the ground) is somehow far worse of a sin than killing the animal in the first place.

People may mistakenly believe that this concept of using all of an animal is why the use of animal body parts in various products is so ubiquitous, but the fact of the matter is that the use of animal body parts is ubiquitous because somewhere, in some way, someone is making a profit. If the parts of those animals are being used in an innovative manner in lieu of being disposed of, it's because someone or some company has figured out a way to turn a profit from those body parts.

Leather is not sold as material to make clothing because the meat and dairy industry didn't want the skin of the cows to go to waste—it's sold because there's money to be made. Leather is considered fashionable, and therefore, it's lucrative.

Leather is only one example of how we use animals for their body parts. Wool, down, beeswax, silk, fur, gelatin, bone char filtration, carmine, castoreum—the list is practically endless. One of the hardest parts about going vegan isn't all the food you have to give up (you don't have to give up any of your favorite foods), but simply avoiding all the products derived from animals. They're everywhere. It takes some time and education, but it's definitely doable.

New vegans often ask "What do I do with my leather/fur/wool/down/silk products after I go vegan?" The answer is it depends on the person. You may decide to keep wearing them or using them until they wear out, not wanting the animal to have suffered in vain. Or you might wear them for a while and then change your mind, realizing that wearing an animal is no longer in alignment with what's in your heart. If you don't want to wear those products anymore, you can donate them, give them to friends, throw them away, or store them somewhere.

Food and fashion isn't the only way animals are used for human benefit. In fact, these may be some of the most "humane" ways humans use animals, if such a thing exists. Not that the life of a factory farmed animal is all fun and games, but it can be argued that animals used for vivisection (scientific experimentation) may be true hell on Earth by comparison. These animals are often kept in cold, dark cages, almost entirely bereft of stimuli, love, or compassion. Many of them endure short, brutal lives of painful experimentation without the use of anesthetics.

Much of the experimentation is done without any real reasoning behind it. When asked the purpose of "injecting radioactive isotopes directly into monkeys' brains" (in his own words), a former laboratory scientist replied "For the purpose of finding out what happens when you inject radioactive isotopes directly into a monkey's brain." In other words, the experimentation wasn't being conducted to ensure a new breakthrough cancer treatment is safe for humans, or to cure some dangerous virus—these experiments were being conducted for the sole purpose of "Hey, let's see what happens!" What's the difference between such experimentation, and, say—a troubled youth putting a puppy in a microwave for the purpose of "Hey, let's see what happens!"?

Assuming the animals are being experimented on for a "good reason" does that make it acceptable? What constitutes a good reason? Many companies test their products on animals but the public will never know the reasons or the nature of the testing. Vegans seek to avoid all products tested on animals, but this is difficult because there are so many. The more we learn and grow as vegans, the more we find other, non-exploitative ways to continue to use the products we need and live the lives we desire. By purchasing and using alternative products and companies, we cast our votes via our dollars. The following is a partial list of companies that have been reported to test on animals. If you're unable to avoid all products offered by all of these companies, don't worry, no one's perfect.

- 3M
- Acuvue
- AirWick
- Almay
- Aquafresh

- Arm & Hammer
- ArmorAll
- Aveeno
- Band-Aid
- Bic
- ChapStick
- Clean & Clear
- Clorox
- Colgate
- Comet
- Coppertone
- CoverGirl
- Crest
- Dial
- Dove
- Downey
- Febreze
- Garnier
- Glad
- Glade
- Gillette
- Head & Shoulders
- Herbal Essences
- Ivory
- Johnson & Johnson

- Lactaid
- Listerine
- Lubriderm
- Lysol
- Maybelline
- Merck
- Mr. Clean
- Neosporin
- Neutrogena
- OFF!
- Olay
- Old Spice
- Oral-B
- Palmolive
- Pampers
- Pantene
- Pledge
- Pine-Sol
- Ponds
- Proctor & Gamble
- Puffs
- Purell
- Raid
- Redken
- Rembrandt

- Revlon
- Right Guard
- Rogaine
- Secret
- Scope
- Splenda
- St. Ives
- Stayfree
- Sudafed
- Tide
- Tommy Hilfiger
- Tylenol
- Unilever
- Vaseline
- Vicks
- Vidal Sassoon
- Visine
- Windex
- Woolite
- Zyrtec

Keep in mind this is only a short, partial list of companies that test on animals. You may be thinking it's impossible to avoid all products by all these companies and so many more that aren't listed here. While it would be difficult, and may *seem* impossible at first glance, many vegans are able to successfully avoid most, if not all, products made by these companies.

While there are many companies that test on animals, the list of companies that DO NOT test on animals is growing. Vegan small businesses are popping up all over the world. Many are still in their infancy and have not yet grown enough or do not have the marketing clout to become household names or to make this list. So check your local businesses, vegfests, co-ops, health food stores, and more health-conscious supermarkets like Whole Foods and Trader Joe's for vegan health and hygiene products. Companies that supposedly do not test on animals include:

- 365
- Alba Botanica
- Aveda
- Anastasia Beverly Hills
- Bath & Body Works
- Biokleen
- Bulldog Natural Skincare
- Cargo Cosmetics
- China Glaze
- Clean Well
- ColourPop
- Cover FX

- Dermalogica
- Desert Essence
- Drybar
- E.L.F. Cosmetics
- Earth Friendly Products
- EcoTools
- Flower
- Glossier
- Hard Candy Cosmetics
- Herbivore Botanicals
- IT Cosmetics
- Jordana
- Josie Maran Cosmetics
- Juice Beauty
- Kat Von D Beauty
- Kiss My Face
- Lavanila
- Lime Crime
- Lush
- Manic Panic
- Method
- Milani
- Mineral Fusion
- Nature's Gate
- Not Your Mother's

- Nudestix
- NYX Cosmetics
- One Love Organics
- Oribe
- Orly
- Pacifica
- Pangea Organics
- Paul Mitchell
- Physician's Formula
- Pixi Beauty
- Red Apple Lipstick
- Renpure
- Skyn Iceland
- Smashbox Cosmetics
- Sonya Dakar
- Sun Bum
- Tarte Cosmetics
- The Body Shop
- Tocca
- Too Faced
- Trader Joe's
- Urban Decay
- W3LL PEOPLE
- Wet n Wild
- Zoya

Expect this list to grow as more vegan and cruelty free companies arrive onto the scene. Many of these companies may be less well-known than most of the companies that do test on animals, but that's not to suggest their products are inferior in any way—all it means is that they are newer companies that aren't as well-established, and they may still lack the marketing clout of the larger companies. That could change in time as the general public grows more aware of animal testing.

Scientific experimentation is only one of many ways that animals are used and exploited for human benefit. Animals are also used as a form of entertainment. You may be thinking about such forms of "entertainment" as bullfighting, dog fighting, cockfighting, horse racing, and dog racing. As awful as those are, how about the more acceptable and perhaps more common ways in which we use animals to entertain us? You may not have considered that the animals in rodeos and circuses are often abused and forced to perform against their will. Have you ever looked into the eyes of a tiger or an elephant performing in the circus? Their eyes reflect the sadness and emptiness in their soul. The life of a circus animal is unpleasant and unnatural. They are kept in small cages when not being trained. They are forced to perform tricks over and over, and are often met with physical abuse or food deprivation when they disobey.

Circus animals are often trained by inflicting pain. The fear of more pain to follow is used to manipulate them into performing. In the case of circus elephants, they are violently abused with bullhooks to the point where the very sight of a bullhook if enough to manipulate them due to their desire to avoid further pain. Avoidance of pain is a powerful motivator, but the catch is that it only works when plain has been inflicted to begin with.

There are other ways in which we use and exploit animals that most people never consider. Take animal riding for example. Horse riding, camel riding, elephant riding— many people don't see these acts as abusive toward animals, but why is that? Is it because of the large size of these animals? Does the fact that they are large in comparison to humans make it acceptable to ride them? Is size the only factor at play here? What if you wanted to ride a dog or a cat? The harm that our weight may cause smaller animals may be obvious, but who is to say a horse or a camel doesn't experience pain when ridden? If we assume there is no pain to the animal, does that make it acceptable? These animals have not given their consent to be ridden, especially in the case when these rides are being offered for money. The owners care little for the wellbeing of these animals beyond their continued ability to give rides and draw in more cash. Forcing animals to do things (against their will, usually in exchange for money) that benefit the animal owners more than the animals themselves—is that not the definition of exploitation?

exploitation (noun):
the action or fact of treating someone
unfairly in order to benefit from their work

It certainly appears to be. To horse owners, horse riding may seem more of an "act of bonding" than exploitation, but why do we not bond with other animals by riding them? Horses do not exist solely for humans to ride. There are other ways to bond with a horse. There is an excellent book on this topic titled 'Riding on the Power of Others: A Horsewoman's Path to Unconditional Love', by Ren Hurst. The book is an excellent read for anyone wishing to follow the path of veganism beyond diet alone.

Zoos tend to be another aspect of human and animal interaction that creates differing opinions. Some people think zoos offer refuge to animals that may be threatened or endangered, and while that may be true, that doesn't mean it's the best way to help these animals. Indeed, the best way to help such animals would be to take better precautions to ensure their survival in the wild. Many threatened or endangered animals got that way due to the actions of humans.

Take the passenger pigeon[13], for example. Once gracing the skies of North America by the billions (yes, *billions*), passenger pigeons have been extinct since 1914, when the last known individual, Martha[14], died at the Cincinnati Zoo. Believed to exist in vast, steady numbers for nearly 20,000 years, the passenger pigeon was almost entirely wiped off the face of the Earth between the years 1800 and 1890. By 1914, they *were* wiped off the face of the Earth. What happened? Humans. Due to deforestation and unabated hunting (aided in several ways by the transcontinental railroad) over many decades, the species was reduced from billions to one lone bird: Martha. Passenger pigeons were hunted mercilessly for meat and to keep them away from crops. The American bison nearly met a similar fate.

Conservation efforts and keeping the birds in zoos could have, in theory, saved the passenger pigeon from extinction, but the fact remains that the reason their numbers were decimated to begin with was that they were hunted without mercy. Hunted for food, for sport, for the preservation of crops, for beds made from their feathers.

Conservation efforts may not have been able to save the passenger pigeon, but a healthy respect for their lives would have prevented them from being hunted to extinction. Unfortunately, that respect did not exist. Keeping and breeding animals in zoos is akin to putting a Band-Aid on a bullet wound: it's often too little, too late. If we wish to save threatened and endangered species from extinction, we must curtail the selfish actions that led them to such a grim fate to begin with.

Zoos, for the most part, are animal prisons. They may be benefitting some species to some degree, but for the vast majority of animals held in zoos, they are little more than prisoners for profit. Zoo animals are confined in spaces that are often many times smaller than the area they'd inhabit in the wild. It's been estimated that zoos provide lions and tigers up to 18,000 times less space, and polar bears up to one million times less space[15] than they'd have in their natural habitat. Many animals in zoos suffer from "zoochosis," a frightening psychological condition that affects animals in captivity. Zoochosis can be characterized by repetitive behavior patterns (swaying, pacing, bar biting, excessive grooming, self-mutilation) not seen in animals in the wild. Zoos exist for profit, not animal welfare or conservation.

Animals are not only used for food, clothing, scientific experimentation, and entertainment. One of the oldest uses of animals is for the purpose of labor. It's believed that oxen were first harnessed and put to work plowing fields over 6,000 years ago[16]. Since then many animals have been used as working animals, often in rough conditions for many hours a day, while the fruits of their labor are taken and used for human benefit alone. When the animals can no longer work to their full capacity, they are often killed and replaced. Horses were used as tools of warfare for thousands of years, ending by World War I after armies began to favor tanks and heavy artillery. Elephants were also used as weapons during warfare. In modern times, using animals as tools of war or for plowing fields has mostly been phased out in favor of machinery, though many animals are still exploited as working animals. From donkey, mule, or horse-drawn carriages to slave monkeys used to pick coconuts, humans still use animals for their labor.

In nearly all cases of animal exploitation, alternative means exist with which to accomplish the same goals. As it's unnecessary to consume animals, it's equally unnecessary to exploit them for purposes of fashion, experimentation, entertainment, transportation, or labor. We can all live in harmony with animals and the planet. We can all learn that animals are our friends, not our possessions.

No One's Perfect, Do the Best You Can

Have you ever heard someone say "You can't be 100% vegan!"? Guess what? It's true. They might add that every time you walk down the street or go for a hike in the woods, you step on bugs. That's also true. You probably kill a few dust mites every time you walk across the carpet of your bedroom. Every time you brush your teeth or rinse your mouth with mouthwash, you're killing bacteria. Every time you shower or wash your hands, you're killing germs. What does that mean?

Absolutely nothing.

You can't avoid killing germs when you wash yourself and you can't avoid stepping on bugs when you go for a walk outside. Insects and animals die when harvesting the foods you eat, and somewhere in your house is a product made by a company that has tested on animals at some point. You can't avoid all these things all the time. You can't be 100% vegan. The definition of a vegan is someone who seeks to avoid all harm to animals whenever possible. That's the best anyone can do. Just because no one is 100% vegan doesn't mean they're not vegan. If you're seeking to avoid all harm to animals whenever possible, that's the best you can do. The key words are *whenever possible*. It's not possible to go for a walk down the street or drive your car to work without accidentally killing bugs. There's simply no way to avoid it. There *is*, however, a way to avoid eating a steak for dinner. It's quite simple, in fact. You eat something else. There *is* a way to avoid pouring cow's milk onto your cereal in the morning. That's simple also. All you have to do is pour oat milk or almond milk instead.

When you buy a steak from the supermarket, you're calling for another steak to replace it on the shelf. You're augmenting the demand that will, in turn, cause another cow to be slaughtered. Supply and demand. When you buy a gallon of cow's milk off the shelf, you're calling for more milk to be produced to replace that gallon. In a sense, you're literally *paying* for those cows to be exploited and slaughtered. These actions are quite easy to avoid, as evidenced by the millions of vegans who avoid them on a daily basis. Whether you buy a steak or a pound of dried beans, a gallon of cow's milk, or a gallon of oat milk, those bugs will still be stepped on when you walk and they'll be splattered on your windshield when you drive. Humans, as a species, may not be able to avoid all harm done to other living things, but does that mean we should go ahead and do the most harm? If we can't do zero harm, does that mean we should continue to directly contribute to the billions of animals that are killed each year?

Anyone who has a basic understanding of animal agriculture can tell you that exponentially more bugs (and other animals) are killed in the production of a steak and a gallon of milk than when you walk down the street or drive your car to work. In the same vein, exponentially more plants are killed by raising cows as food than when humans eat plant food directly. Animal agriculture causes *maximum* harm.

Simply because no one is able to cause *zero* harm is no reason to remain indifferent while most of the human race proceeds to cause maximum harm.

While no one can be 100% vegan, by the definition of the word "vegan" we can all seek to do the least amount of harm to animals and this planet. We can all do our best to live in harmony with the beings we share the planet with, and that includes not intentionally forcing them to work for us, not forcing them to perform tricks for us, not conducting experiments on them, not using them for the food they make to feed themselves, and not killing them to eat when it's completely unnecessary. Maybe you can't be 100% vegan because you brush your teeth and step on bugs, but if you could live without directly and intentionally harming animals, why wouldn't you? You can. Anyone can.

You May Not Succeed the First Time

You may not succeed the first time you go vegan. You may last a week, a month, even a year or more and then revert back to being vegetarian or even to an omnivorous diet and lifestyle. To compare going vegan to smoking cessation once more, many people need to try it several times before it sticks. It's not that being vegan is difficult, it's a matter of the lifestyle being so *vastly different* than the lifestyle most of us have lived our entire lives. Most people grew up on meat, milk, cheese, eggs, and honey. Most people grew up wearing leather, wool, sleeping under the warmth of down comforters, using products that were tested on animals, and attending zoos, circuses, and agricultural fairs. Some vegans are former farmers, former hunters, and fishermen. Any great lifestyle shift will create challenges and conflict. What makes the difference is how we respond to those challenges and that conflict.

Many people who go vegan for health reasons alone do not stick with it. Our own personal health is often a weak motivator. This is why many people smoke, drink to excess, use drugs, eat junk food, and fail to engage in frequent exercise despite being well aware of the consequences. Humans are prone to want immediate gratification. That bacon double cheeseburger, extra large order of fries, and large chocolate milkshake tastes so good right now, few of us consider the consequences we may face down the road should we continue to eat such food regularly.

If you want to go vegan and stay vegan, it helps to have more powerful motivators than your own personal health. Health may get you through the door, but it will take more than that to keep you in the room. Staying healthy for your children and the rest of your family is a more powerful motivator than doing it for yourself. The question is, will that be a strong enough motivator to stay the course? Concern for animals, other people, the environment, and the future of this entire planet are much more powerful motivators. Why not go vegan for all these reasons and more?

Regardless of *why* you want to transition to a vegan diet and lifestyle, realize that it may not work the first time. That doesn't mean this diet and lifestyle aren't "for you." All it means is that you're facing some significant life changes and it may take longer to adapt to those changes than you initially expected.

If a vegan diet and lifestyle didn't work for you the first time, don't get down on yourself. Don't let the opinions of others get you down, either. Take some time to regroup and come up with a plan to do it again. The best thing about taking more than one shot at going vegan before it sticks is that you'll learn from it each time. Take a good look at your experience and try to pinpoint what went wrong. Why didn't it work for you the first time around, or the second, or the third? Were you eating enough food? Did you grow tired of eating the same meals over and over? Did you feel isolated because you don't know any other vegans? Did you mistake common detox symptoms for a dangerous vitamin deficiency? Did you find yourself feeling hungry all the time? Did you feel surrounded by people who didn't support your new diet and lifestyle? Spend some time learning about how to overcome the hurdles you faced (we all face our own different challenges when going vegan) and use the insight and the knowledge you've gained with each attempt to help you when you go vegan the next time. As with quitting smoking or any other challenge, it will get easier with each attempt.

Staying Vegan for the Long Run

The focus of this book is transitioning to a vegan diet because it's the number one thing we can do to help prevent the continued harm inflicted on animals. Most of the animals that are killed in this world are killed for food. However, if you wish to stay vegan long-term, focusing on your diet may not be enough. Going vegan for personal health or to try out the next fad diet isn't a strong enough motivator for most people to stay vegan. Focusing on a vegan *lifestyle* is more sustainable because then we have something bigger to motivate us.

If you want to stay vegan indefinitely, it will help to overhaul your lifestyle, how you view animals, and how you interact with them. If you continue to see them as "lesser" beings or commodities to be used and exploited, you may find yourself relying on little more than willpower to stay vegan, and for many of us, willpower isn't enough. If you can consider why you don't hurt dogs or cats and apply those same sentiments to other animals, you'll be in a better position to have the mindset you'll need to stick with it and not miss your old ways.

That said, your own personal health is an important part of the picture. If you neglect your health and become a "junk food" vegan, you'll most likely not be getting all the nutrients your body needs to stay healthy. In time you may develop vitamin deficiencies and eventually you may be tempted to revert back to a vegetarian or omnivorous diet. This happens to many "ex vegans" who come to believe that the missing animal products are what's causing their health to decline. Health will decline on any diet if we're not getting what we need to sustain our bodies.

The key to staying vegan for the long run is finding that balance between your own person health and your concern for the animals and the planet. For many people, either one of these factors alone is not enough.

Another thing that helps sustain a vegan diet and lifestyle is to find a support system. It's much more difficult to make major lifestyle changes when we're entirely alone in our endeavors with no one to offer support when we need it. If you know anyone who has been vegan for decades, they'll attest to how things have changed. Twenty or thirty years ago, vegans were much rarer. Many of us had probably never even heard the term "vegan" twenty or thirty years ago. Anyone you know who has been vegan for that amount of time or longer most likely had a difficult road. It's doubtful they had any vegan friends or support. They had no vegan restaurants, no vegan options, and no convenient vegan food at the supermarket, save for the basics like rice, beans, lentils, oats, and produce.

Times have changed and the movement has grown like many old-school vegans would never have believed. Not only do we have vegan options, vegan restaurants, and shelves stocked with vegan food at the supermarket, we also have other vegans. Take advantage of your local vegan Facebook groups, local vegan festivals, meet-ups, and other gatherings. If you have other vegan friends you can turn to when you're going through a tough time, they'll be able to offer support when you need it the most and you'll be able to offer the same in return. Vegans may be a small percentage of the population, but if you have people to share stories and recipes with, friends to turn to when you're going through a rough patch, you won't feel so alone.

If you can find a vegan mentor, someone who has been vegan for years, to whom you can turn when you have questions or need advice, it will make all the difference when embarking on this journey. It doesn't have to be someone you've known for a long time or even someone you know in person. With the help of the internet, you can find someone half way around the world and it won't matter as long as they have the experience and they're willing to offer their help. The more long-term vegans you can befriend, the better, because then you'll know your finding a long-term vegan wasn't a fluke. Folks who have been vegan for ten years, twenty years, even thirty years or more are out there. The woman who operates the popular Facebook food group What Broke Vegans Eat has been vegan since birth. There's a vegan animal rights activist in Australia who has been vegan since birth in 1956. There's a vegan fitness enthusiast in the United Kingdom who has been vegan since age five in 1957. Many people aren't aware that there's anyone alive who has been vegan for so long because veganism had been so rare for so many years. Not anymore. The movement is growing even more rapidly now, as the information is spreading that it's not necessary to eat or otherwise harm animals anymore. It hasn't been for a long time.

Conclusion

You can transition to vegan lifestyle without giving up your favorite foods or sacrificing anything. You have nothing to lose and so much to gain.

This book was originally meant to help people transition to a vegan diet, but it grew and transformed and became more. Something many vegans do when we realize changing our diets is no longer enough. We realize we not only have the power to make more conscious choices when it comes to our food, but also when it comes to our lives, those around us, and the planet. We have the power to do so much more than simply not eat animals. We have the power to change the way we impact the world as a whole. The power is inside all of us.

Notes

[1] https://www.apexbeecompany.com/honey-bee-facts/

[2] https://www.peta.org/about-peta/faq/which-beers-are-suitable-for-vegans/

[3] https://www.peta.org/about-peta/faq/is-wine-vegan/

[4] https://www.worldwildlife.org/industries/palm-oil

[5] https://faq.impossiblefoods.com/hc/en-us/articles/360019100553-What-is-soy-leghemoglobin-or-heme-

[6] https://www.businessinsider.com/supplements-vitamins-bad-or-good-health-2017-8

[7] https://www.todaysdietitian.com/newarchives/0419p30.shtml

[8] https://www.nhs.uk/conditions/vitamin-b12-or-folate-deficiency-anaemia/causes/

[9] https://fungi.com/blogs/articles/place-mushrooms-in-sunlight-to-get-your-vitamin-d

[10] https://www.vitamindcouncil.org/about-vitamin-d/how-do-i-get-the-vitamin-d-my-body-needs/#.XW2TelYpC1s

[11] https://www.vegan.com/omega-3/

[12] https://www.vrg.org/nutrition/iodine_diet.php

[13] https://en.wikipedia.org/wiki/Passenger_pigeon

[14] https://en.wikipedia.org/wiki/Martha_(passenger_pigeon)

[15] https://www.freedomforanimals.org.uk/zoos

[16] https://en.wikipedia.org/wiki/Ox

Made in the
USA
Middletown, DE

77035769R00096